Bedding Plants

Prolonging Shelf Performance

Grateful acknowledgement for photos is given to Ball Seed Co., especially Lisa Segroves; Fischer Geraniums U.S.A., Inc. for Brazil geranium; *FloraCulture International* magazine; Goldsmith Seeds, Inc. for Peter Pan zinnia; *GrowerTalks* magazine; and PanAmerican Seed Co. for Wizard Mix coleus and Easter Bonnet Mix lobularia.

Cover photo courtesy PanAmerican Seed Co.

Bedding Plants

Prolonging Shelf Performance

Postproduction Care & Handling

Allan M. Armitage

Ball Publishing

Batavia, Illinois USA

Ball Publishing
335 N. River Street
P.O. Box 9
Batavia, Illinois 60510 USA

Printed in the United States of America.

98 97 96 95 94 93   5 4 3 2 1

Ohio State University hopes that users of this book will find it useful
and informative. While the author has endeavored to provide accurate
information, Ohio State University asks users to call its attention to
any errors. The author has attempted to obtain information included
in this book from reliable sources; however, the accuracy and
completeness of this book and any opinion based thereon are not
guaranteed. No endorsement is intended for products mentioned, nor
is criticism meant for products not mentioned.

Library of Congress Cataloging in Publication Data
Armitage, A. M. (Allan M.)
    Bedding plants : prolonging shelf performance : postproduction
    care & handling / Allan M. Armitage.
        p.   cm.
    Includes bibliographical references and index.

    ISBN 0-9626796-6-6 : $37.00.
    1. Bedding plants—Handling.   2. Bedding plants—Postharvest
       technology   I. Title.
SB431.A75 1993   92-45175
635.9'626—dc20   CIP

CONTENTS

FOREWORD

Bedding Plants: Prolonging Shelf Performance is one of a series of four books about the care and handling of plants from the grower to the consumer. It's designed to give the entire marketing-user chain of grower, wholesaler, retail outlet and consumer the current recommendations on the most effective procedures for each postproduction stage—as each has its own specific considerations.

We may think of using colorful flowers outdoors for enjoyment during warm weather as a more modern custom, but it's actually a tradition dating back for many years. In Victorian times, for example, complex designs were created outdoors and in conservatories with mostly tropical herbaceous perennials. The plants were grown from cuttings taken late in the growing season, overwintered in greenhouses, replanted, fertilized and pruned until they could be bedded out the next year. Since the desired flower colors and plant forms didn't come true from seed, asexual propagation of cuttings was the only way to create specific, desired displays.

Beginning in the 1930s, breeding bedding plants entered the modern era. Horticultural scientists learned how to select, cross-fertilize and create a whole new generation of bedding plants with wider ranges of colors, forms, habits, disease and insect resistance and performance. Not only was it possible to grow the plants from seed, but all of the production techniques—climate control, soilless mixes, sterile containers, and pest control measures—were perfected. Today, bedding plants are the most rapidly

growing segment of the Green Industries. The plants flower so heavily and so persistently that you can't see any foliage—all you see are flowers. These developments have added broader plant lists to use, a longer performance season and now with the introduction of perennials grown from seed, a more flexible management program. This book deals with the specific requirements for the postproduction care and handling of bedding plants. We hope you'll find that the successful practice of such care begins here.

The Postproduction series includes the following four books: *Bedding Plants: Prolonging Shelf Performance* by Allan M. Armitage, University of Georgia; *Cut Flowers: Prolonging Freshness (2nd ed.)* by John N. Sacalis, Rutgers University, and edited by Joseph L. Seals; *Flowering Potted Plants: Prolonging Shelf Performance* by Terril A. Nell, University of Florida; and *Foliage Plants: Prolonging Quality* by Thomas M. Blessington, University of Maryland, and Pamela C. Collins, landscape design and interior plantscaping consultant.

These four postproduction books originated from the series produced through the Kiplinger Chair in Horticulture at The Ohio State University, Columbus, Ohio. During 1980-1981, I occupied the Kiplinger Chair, which is funded by businesses, foundations and individuals to support research and educational activities for floricultural excellence. The Chair honors Dr. D.C. Kiplinger, professor of floriculture, for his contributions as a teacher, researcher and extension specialist. Recommendations for the Chair urged expanded research in production and distribution of high quality floral products, and postproduction books on bedding plants, cut flowers, flowering potted plants and foliage plants were subsequently planned and produced by the Kiplinger Chair.

Committee members during the creation of the guides were: Stanley F. Backman, Minneapolis, MN; Roger D. Blackwell, Columbus, OH; H. Marc Cathey, Beltsville, MD; for the Ohio Florists Association: Willard H. Barco, Medina, OH, James F. Bridenbaugh, Kent, OH and August J.

Corso, Sandusky, OH; Paul Ecke Jr., Encinitas, CA; Harry K. Tayama, Columbus, OH; and for The Ohio State University: Robert A. Kennedy, Steven M. Still and Luther Waters Jr.

H. Marc Cathey
National Chair for Florist
    and Nursery Crops Review
U.S. Department of Agriculture
Washington, DC

INTRODUCTION

T he wholesale value of bedding plants (flowering flats, flowering pots and vegetables) was conservatively estimated to be $840 million in 1990 and continues to increase. Outlets for bedding plant sales include florists, grocery stores, mass market outlets, hardware stores, nurseries, garden clubs and even gasoline/food stores. In recent years there has been a steady demand for annuals, while perennial plant and herb sales are also increasing at a dizzying rate.

The bullish market for bedding plants, however, has resulted in too many growers cutting corners to produce plants at a low price for the discount market, too many outlets staffed by people wholly unqualified to care for even the best grown plants and too many consumers buying an inferior product requiring time to become established in the garden. Such shortcomings, without a doubt, will lead to both retailers and consumers losing confidence in the product. *This potential loss of confidence in our product is the single most important factor that can undermine the floricultural industry.*

It's estimated that due to poor handling, 20% of floricultural products become unsalable, damaged or reduced in price after grower production. Seasonal plant losses at mass market outlets can be staggering: The consumer blames the retailer, the retailer blames the grower, who in turn accuses the retailer of poor handling practices.

Who then is to blame for such losses? Surely no other industry in this country could assume such enormous losses year after year and still remain healthy. If the car, textile or fast food industries encountered

such losses, significant time and money would be expended trying to correct the causes. Each car manufacturer, textile dealer and fast food franchiser would recognize that a problem existed, study the problem and then do whatever was necessary to minimize it. Failure to recognize that a 20% loss is a problem is unintelligent. Not to attempt to reduce it is financial suicide. The garden plant industry is similar to other industries with their diverse and independent members. Blaming one another is comparable to arguing about who set fire to the curtains. By the time you have the answer, it's too late to save the house.

The bedding plant and perennial plant industry is healthy in spite of its problems, but it cannot become complacent. All segments of the floricultural chain—growers, shippers, retailers and consumers—have a responsibility to reduce losses. Each influences the overall health of the plant. Once it leaves the production area, the combined efforts of all segments have a significant influence on plants' postproduction longevity.

What can an individual business do to help reduce these losses? The answer depends on the job being done, but through the whole cycle from production to sale, the one constant is the plant. When the plant is in the greenhouse, its environment is ideal. When it leaves the greenhouse, it will be subjected to stress. The questions then are "How can the plant be prepared for future stress?" and "How can that stress be reduced?"

This guide has been written in two parts to answer these basic questions. The first part, postproduction factors, explains the general concepts and practices that the producer, shipper, retailer and consumer can implement. This part is by far the most important because understanding the relationship of plant longevity to growing and handling methods provides the building blocks for increasing individual species' longevity. The second part consists of specific recommendations and comments concerning individual crops (species) based on what is known about them through past and current research. Unfortunately, little research has been conducted on bedding plant postproduction problems in general. In fact, less than 5% of the numerous research papers, trade journal articles or extension publications written about postproduction care of floricultural products deals with bedding plant species. The situation is even worse for perennial species. Large gaps exist in our knowledge, but what is known is presented in the Crops section.

POSTPRODUCTION FACTORS

Five major factors affect postproduction bedding plants' longevity:

1. **The plant's genetic makeup: The breeder's responsibility**

2. **Production area: The grower's responsibility**

3. **Shipping and transportation: The shipper's and trucker's responsibility**

4. **Retail area: The retail management's responsibility**

5. **Garden area: The consumer's responsibility**

The plant's genetic makeup: *The breeder's responsibility*

Floriculture crop breeding programs have placed little emphasis on selecting for better shelf life. The exceptions may be in cut roses, but I know of no work in bedding plant breeding where breeders are specifically looking for better postproduction performance in retail environments. Obvious differences in shelf life occur among chrysanthemum and poinsettia cultivars, and it's likely that similar differences exist among the many cultivars in bedding plant species. One reason why cultivar selection for durable retail shelf life is a minor breeding priority is that bedding plants are planted outdoors. It's assumed that only a short time lapses between production and sale, but unfortunately this isn't always the case. In many retail outlets, 5 to 10 days may elapse between shipment and sale. Presently, there aren't many bedding plants with long shelf lives to choose from. In the future, there may even be fewer cultivars available to consumers because, rightly or wrongly, bedding plant breeders have chosen to emphasize other aspects of plant production.

The responsibility, then, for increasing postproduction quality falls upon other segments of the production, transport and retail chain. All serious flower breeders, however, are strongly committed to enhancing garden performance, certainly an important part of postproduction. Many cultivars today show superior garden performance compared with their predecessors, a major step in the right direction.

Production area: *The grower's responsibility*

Overall plant quality

At certain times in the production cycle, decisions influencing longevity need to be made, but what about day-to-day activities such as watering, fertilizing and applying chemicals? Many specific activities at the end of the production phase can be tailored to increase shelf life, and these will be discussed later in more detail. *Any practice, however, that decreases plant quality during production, also decreases shelf life.* Such things as leaf chlorosis, marginal foliar burn, insects and/or disease, poor root growth or physiological disorders all reduce plant quality. Regardless of the causes, a plant suffering stress has a reduced shelf life. If poor quality plants leave the greenhouse, then the best display/retail area in the world will not improve their postproduction life.

In this manual, the reader can assume that good quality plants are being produced, shipped, stored or sold. Techniques to increase longevity of bedding plants will be discussed later in this section.

Sowing date

Early production decisions influence plants' shelf life. The grower's decision concerning sowing time has a bearing on postproduction life even before a seed packet is opened. Early sowing yields plants ready for the early spring market when temperatures are cooler—a factor increasing shelf life even under poor retail conditions. Late sowings, on the other hand, result in plants being subjected to much warmer temperatures, often leading to their rapid decline. Sowing time is dictated by the marketplace; the later the sowing, however, the greater potential for losses, particularly if the final container size, which is determined by sowing time, remains the same throughout.

Container size

The warmer the temperatures that plants are exposed to, the faster the water loss and the more rapid the plant's decline. Larger soil volumes increase longevity (Table 1), a fact even more evident under late season conditions.

All containers in the study were 2 inches (5 cm) in diameter, as are many cell packs. Even a 1-inch (½-cm) increase in depth significantly delayed the onset of wilting without increased bench space. Not all species tested responded similarly to the additional 1-inch depth, but all bedding

Table 1
Container size affects plant wilting time

Container depth (inches)	Marigold		Salvia	
	Shelf life (hours)	Increase over control (%)	Shelf life (hours)	Increase over control (%)
2	94	-	96	-
3	116	23	116	22
4	129	37	136	41
5	138	47	152	58

Source: Adapted from Gehring and Lewis (1979a,c).

plants persist longer with greater soil volume. One of the greatest mistakes made by the bedding plant industry regarding shelf life was adopting the 2¼-inch deep cell pack as an unofficial standard. These shallow cells are fine if we assume plants will be watered as well in the retail environment as they are during production. That's an assumption that simply doesn't happen in "real life." In many retail outlets, personnel aren't trained to water properly, and the environments in which plants are placed often cause greater water loss. If plants will be finished in cell packs, it makes sense to plant them in as large a space as economically feasible. The extra soil in a 36 cell pack compared with a 72 cell pack may increase shelf life enough to warrant the extra cost (Table 2).

Table 2
Soil volume and cost[1]

No. of cavities	Soil volume per cavity (ml)	Cost of soil per cavity[2]
18	300	2.5 cents
24	200	1.7 cents
36	150	1.2 cents
48	100	0.8 cents
72	75	0.6 cents

1. Based on cavity size (standard 11" x 22" cell pack).
2. Premixed 3 cu. ft. bag at $7.

There's no doubt that late sowings should be finished in larger containers than early sowings. The additional built-in shelf life through one larger container can also provide an excellent marketing advantage for plants grown from late season sowings.

The recent trend towards larger, deeper containers (3-inch [7-cm] or more) is an excellent move toward improving shelf life. Not only do plants last longer in the retail sales area, but the larger size also promotes faster development in the landscape. Unfortunately, many of the larger containers are sold directly to landscapers and are bypassing the retail area. Most plants sold to mass market outlets are still produced in smaller containers.

Growing media

An artificial growing medium's main function is to maximize root growth which, in turn, aids the plant's top growth. A good medium does this by containing a proper ratio of air to water space, a good nutrient uptake by the roots, adequate water-holding capacity and adequate drainage (although aeration and drainage are also closely related to container depth—the shallower the container, the poorer the aeration and drainage). Essentially, however, a good medium must sustain good growth. Today, there are almost as many media mixes on the market for both plugs and containers as there are growers. In this section, we'll look at various media, the still-existing debate as to media's importance and the effectiveness of adding hydrogel to media.

When peat-lite (50:50 peat:vermiculite) was compared to noncomposted shredded hardwood bark mix, research showed that bark mix held slightly more available water, and plants had a better shelf life, measured by time until wilt (Table 3).

Table 3
Plant media's effect on wilting time

Crop	Media	Available water (%)	Days to wilt
Chrysanthemum	Peat/perlite	39	7
	Bark	41	8½
Easter lily	Peat/perlite	32	6½
	Bark	35	7

Source: Adapted from Bearce and McCollum.

Although these aren't bedding plants being evaluated, the data prove that some growing media may be better adapted for reducing the effects of prolonged stress in retail conditions. Both these crops were grown in 6-inch (15-cm) pots, a very different situation than for plants grown in cell packs.

Some debate still exists as to media's importance. Research work with petunias (36 per pack) showed no difference in production or shelf life quality after 15 days comparing three different growing media commonly used in greenhouse production (Table 4).

Table 4
Artificial media's effect on petunia shelf life*

	1:1:1 Soil:Peat:Vermiculite	1:1 Peat:Vermiculite	3:1 Vermiculite:Peat
Day 5	4.9	4.9	4.8
Day 10	3.9	4.0	3.9
Day 15	2.9	2.9	3.0

* Based on visual rating (5=excellent; 1=poor).
Source: Adapted from Armitage (1986a).

All plants were subjected to similar light, temperature and humidity levels. Only three mixes were tested; many more exist. Similar results with six other species also showed no differences among peat-lite-based mixes after 12 days in the postproduction environment. If plants were held for 36 days, however, differences between soil and soilless media were apparent in impatiens, petunia and tomato. In general, if the media enhances plants' quality in the greenhouse, it probably won't detract from plants' retail shelf life.

Has the trend towards soilless growing media affected shelf life? That question was addressed by the Connecticut Greenhouse Crop Production Task Force more than a decade ago, and the task force suggested adding 10% to 20% soil to peat-lite root media. Research at Cornell University verified the Connecticut group's position by proving that soil-based media did, in fact, benefit chrysanthemum's shelf life (Table 5).

Table 5
Using soil benefits chrysanthemum's shelf life*

Cultivar	Peat-lite	Peat-lite + 20% soil	Soil:Peat:Perlite (1:1:1 volume)
Mandalay	22	22	24
Mountain Peak	23	27	28
Capri	14	22	23

* Visual rating in days. Source: Adapted from Boodley et al.

If shelf life data for each cultivar is averaged for the two growing media containing soil and compared with the peat-lite mix, increases of 4.5%, 19.5% and 37.8% occurred with Mandalay, Mountain Peak and Capri respectively. All plants were grown in 6-inch [15-cm] pots; a limited number of plants was used. The large differences between cultivars do not permit extrapolation to other species or container sizes, but it's certainly plausible that adding soil improves water-holding capacity and aids longevity. Realistically, however, it's doubtful the greenhouse industry will ever revert to soil-based mixes and certainly not in bedding plant production. Everything possible must be done throughout the postproduction chain to reduce plant stress and improve the environment in which plants are grown and sold.

Amending the mix with hydrogel. Hydrophilic polymers (generically referred to as hydrogels) are substances that absorb 20 to 50 times their weight in water. Most of the materials act as rechargeable reservoirs, making absorbed water available to plant roots on demand. Hydrogels have been used successfully to reduce wilting and decrease the watering frequency in outdoor landscapes, hanging baskets, interior plants and potted plants. At present they are most commonly used in floriculture as soil amendments for hanging baskets.

There are many conflicting opinions on hydrogel's benefit. Studies of pilea, maranta and chrysanthemum found significant delays in wilting time using different soil mixes. When analyzing bedding plants grown in standard 72 per cell flats, Gehring and Lewis found that plants with the recommended hydrogel rate delayed wilting by an average 27% over those with no hydrogel (Table 6).

Table 6
Hydrogel's influence on bedding plant shelf life

Hydrogel concentration (kg per m³)	Ageratum		Zinnia	
	Shelf life (hours)	Increase over control (%)	Shelf life (hours)	Increase over control (%)
Control	85	-	79	-
4	97	14	103	30
8	113	33	124	57
12	120	40	135	71

Source: Adapted from Gehring (1979b).

This test was conducted under laboratory conditions with the temperature maintained at approximately 70°F (21°C). Under actual marketing conditions, the improvement in shelf life may be less. There were no apparent differences in the hydrogel's effectiveness in larger containers. While many research studies have shown hydrogel's beneficial effects, some reports contradict the positive results. Hydrogel's absorbency and media water retention, however, are sharply reduced by iron-containing fertilizers such as iron sulfate or Micromax; also free calcium and magnesium reduce hydrogel's effectiveness. This means that adding many plant nutrients reduces hydrogel efficiency. The problem, however, can be solved by providing chelated forms of iron, calcium and magnesium. Some studies showed little difference in shelf life (measured by visual rating) in petunias grown in 36 cells per pack, in marigolds, or in plants placed in warm conditions. The sum of these experiments indicates hydrogels may be useful in delaying wilting time in container-grown crops, but may be only slightly beneficial in prolonging visual quality in standard cell packs under stressful conditions. There are, however, no instances where commercially available hydrogels damaged any crops when applied at recommended rates. Adding hydrogel won't hurt, and will likely extend, the shelf life of 4-inch (10-cm) potted or hanging basket bedding plants.

Growth regulators

Growers' rationale for using growth regulators such as Cycocel, B-Nine, A-Rest, Ethrel, Bonzi, Sumagic and others is to improve visual quality and simplify shipping pots or bedding plant flats. Growth regulators, however, also enhance shelf life in two ways:

(1) Growth regulators such as Cycocel and Bonzi significantly increase plants' chlorophyll content, which enhances photosynthesis and results in less stress-susceptible plants.

(2) Plants that are compact due to growth regulator applications are less prone to physical damage and tolerate rough handling in a bouncing truck or from gardeners' hungry hands in retail shopping centers. Reduced plant size results in reduced water loss and less stress under unfavorable conditions. From a postproduction point of view, this is growth regulators' greatest benefit. When petunias were sprayed with one or two applications of B-Nine, the amount of water lost for every inch of plant was the same as those not sprayed (Table 7).

Because the treated plants were shorter and more compact, however, less total water was lost and wilting was delayed.

Table 7
B-Nine's effect on postproduction petunia water loss

	Height at flowering (inches)	Water loss (grams)	Water loss per inch of height
No B-Nine	7.3	225	30.8
One B-Nine application	6.1	201	32.9
Two B-Nine applications	5.7	184	32.2

Source: Adapted from Wise (1980).

If plants are naturally compact, shelf life won't be enhanced by applying growth regulator. A great deal of information relating to application, dosage and frequency of growth regulators for production purposes is available, however, and it's a comforting thought that applying growth regulators to enhance quality production also enhances postproduction life.

Toning plants

Toning is simply the practice of preparing a plant for a different environment. The need for toning or crop acclimatization likely arose from plants declining in retail outlets where conditions drastically differed from those in production areas. In the quest for the fastest flowering time, crops are provided with warm temperatures, high fertility rates and constant irrigation throughout the crop cycle to reduce bench time. Faster flowering cultivars and technological advances in production such as constant liquid feed systems, boom watering and sub-flat heating systems have not only allowed more critical control of energy, water and fertilizer but have also pushed the crops to maturity as rapidly as possible. In most bedding plant production manuals, there's little emphasis on crop toning. Yet, if plants fall apart at the retail outlet because of lack of toning, repeat sales for next year's fast crop may be slow in coming.

Toning isn't difficult. It is short-term, and it saves money. It must, however, be scheduled into the production cycle, and crops must be arranged in the greenhouse so the proper environment can be provided. There are three types of toning: temperature toning, fertility toning and light intensity toning.

Temperature toning. In general, most bedding plants are grown at relatively warm temperatures (60° to 80°F [16° to 27°C] depending on season and species). It's well-known that cool temperatures slow growth and flowering while warm temperatures accelerate them. Reducing night temperatures prior to shipping (when the flower bud becomes visible) adds additional shelf life to many bedding plant species. For example, when marigolds were grown at 50°, 60° or 70°F (10°, 16° or 21°C) night temperature, from visible bud until market, those held at 50°F had the longest shelf life (Table 8).

Table 8
Lowering production temperature affects marigold shelf life

Retail temperature	Days marketable at production night temperature		
	50°F	60°F	70°F
50°F	17	14	12
70°F	17	13	10
90°F	4	4	4
Source: Adapted from Nelson et al. (1980).			

Notice that at 70°F (21°C) retail temperature, marigolds lasted seven days longer after being toned at 50°F (10°C) greenhouse temperature, compared with a 70°F greenhouse temperature. This also dramatically illustrates the retail temperature's effect on postproduction life. (See discussion in the retail section.) Impatiens, however, did not react the same (Table 9).

Table 9
Lowering production temperature affects impatiens shelf life

Retail temperature	Days marketable at production night temperature		
	50°F	60°F	70°F
50°F	12	15	10
70°F	13	15	15
90°F	2	2	2
Source: Adapted from Nelson et al. (1980).			

Because impatiens is a warmth-loving species, compared to marigold (first frost kills impatiens but not marigold), these results aren't unexpected. Not all crops can be temperature toned in the same manner, but two groups are identifiable (Table 10).

Table 10
Bedding plants' tolerance of cool night temperatures

Group A Temperature toned	Group B Temperature toned
at 50° to 55°F	at 58° to 62°F
Ageratum	Begonia
Alyssum	Celosia
Calendula	Coleus
Dianthus	Impatiens
Marigold	Pepper
Pansy	Tomato
Petunia	Vinca (catharanthus)
Perennials (all)	Zinnia
Phlox	
Salvia	
Snapdragon	
Torenia	

For plants in Group A, lowering temperature results in significantly less respiration and a subsequent carbohydrate buildup essential for stress tolerance. Those in Group B are more tender, and lowering temperatures to 50°F (10°C) for a prolonged time does more harm than good.

Fertility toning. Little work has been done with bedding plant crops to determine a fertility program's effect on shelf life.

Should fertilization be continued throughout the entire production schedule, or should it be increased, decreased or discontinued altogether near the end of the production cycle to prepare for the postproduction environment?

Fertilizer concentration shouldn't be increased prior to shipping. Giving one last "shot for the road" only provides additional soft growth and a greater potential for salt damage when plants dry out (which they invariably will). Discontinuing fertilizer entirely is also a poor practice because of soilless media's low nutrient pool (in soil culture, much more is available over a longer period of time). The best practice is to reduce fertilizer rates near the end of the crop cycle. Not enough is known to say exactly how much reduction and how soon, but Table 11 shows what happens with petunias after 10 days.

Table 11
Effect of reducing or discontinuing fertilizer at visible bud stage

Reducing fertilizer from 200 ppm to:	Visual rating*
200 (no change)	3.3
100	4.2
0	2.9

* Data taken at 10 days; 5=excellent, 1=poor.
Source: Adapted from Armitage (1986a).

These data show that reducing fertilizer from 200 ppm to 100 ppm when flower buds were visible resulted in better looking plants after 10 days in retail conditions. In some cases, no differences were noted between plants maintained at 200 ppm and those reduced to 100 ppm at visible bud, but in no case was fertilizer reduction detrimental to shelf life. Here, then, is a practice that saves money and is good for the plant as well. Eliminating fertilizer entirely isn't a good idea, at least for petunias. For plants with lower sensitivity to soluble salts, and those with less time between visible bud and open flower (for example, impatiens), discontinuing fertilizer entirely at visible bud stage

would likely have little effect on shelf life. In general, however, reducing fertilizer concentration by 50% at the visible bud stage is a smart practice.

Light intensity toning. In general, the value of toning bedding plants by reducing light intensity is questionable. Reducing bedding plant light prior to shipping reduces carbohydrates and appears to have no benefit, but little work has been done to test this point. Bedding plants that will be shipped for more than 3 days in the dark may benefit from reduced light in the greenhouse, as do perennials and foliage plants. Some potted plants and many foliage species may benefit from reduced light in the production phase—foliage plants' ultimate destination is indoors, where light intensities are low relative to the production area—so it makes sense to reduce light intensity for them, but not for bedding plants. With bedding plants, toning is done simply to make them tough enough to tolerate a stressful retail setting prior to begin planted outdoors.

Irrigation

The way plants are watered can significantly affect not only bench time and crop quality but also postproduction life. Plants kept constantly moist are taller, with longer internodes, but may weigh no more than those allowed to occasionally dry out. On the other hand, plants allowed to dry to the point of visible wilting require more bench time and are often poorer quality. Reducing irrigation frequency to tone plants should be done near the crop cycle's end.

The following experiment shows watering frequency effects under simulated warm (68°F [20°C] constant) and hot (68°F [20°C] nights, 90°F [32°C] days) retail areas. In both retail simulations, overwatered plant damage showed up rapidly during postproduction, but those same plants looked fine on the bench! These data clearly indicate that plants should be allowed to dry at the production cycle's end, but not to the point of obvious, prolonged wilting. It's difficult to recommend exactly when to start reducing water, but the visible bud stage seems most appropriate. This practice will not slow flowering down (the process of flower opening is mostly dependent on temperature), yet it will harden the plant off for the rigors to come.

Table 12
Lower irrigation frequency lengthens plant life in warm/hot environments

Frequency of watering	Warm area (Days)	Hot area (Days)
High	9	4
"Normal"	9	6
Low	15	8

Source: Adapted from Armitage and Kowalski (1983b).

Using antitranspirants

One of the greatest postproduction environment concerns is excessive water loss. Applying an antitranspirant chemical to plants' foliage when they are ready to be shipped is a potential way to reduce water loss. Antitranspirants have been used with cineraria and hydrangea, which have high rates of transpiration, but they aren't widely used in the floriculture industry. Studying antitranspirant use as a postproduction aid, Gehring and Lewis couldn't show significant increases in shelf life of any bedding plant tested when they used two chemicals at three different rates and compared them with untreated plants. A later study also found antitranspirants had little benefit in increasing petunias' shelf life. This doesn't mean that antitranspirants are of no use in increasing shelf life, but they appear of minor value compared with other less costly practices.

Final grooming

One of the most important production jobs is simply good business: grooming plants prior to shipping. Removing dead or dying tissue—leaves, buds and flowers—not only makes plants more attractive but also sharply reduces the dying tissue's production of ethylene gas. Ethylene promotes bud abscission, and if enough is present, also causes leaf drop in some bedding plants. During the busy shipping season, plants will inevitably be mishandled and abused, so it's essential that someone inspect all plants before the flats leave the greenhouse. This is your plants' final journey, and they should go "well dressed."

Plugs vs. finished plants

Started plants grown in small single units—plugs—also cycle through a definite postproduction phase. After 4 to 6 weeks of production, many are shipped to another grower for finishing.

The shipping phase is the plug material's postproduction phase. Readying these plants for shipping is also the grower's responsibility.

All the steps mentioned previously in the grower program for increasing finished plants' shelf life are also appropriate for plug flats shipped from greenhouse to greenhouse. The only difference is that plugs have to tolerate shipping stress, not retail environment stress. Major points to consider for plugs are container volume and plant toning by reducing water and fertilizer. Reducing temperature should not be practiced. Plugs won't "take off" as rapidly in the final container if they've endured a week of cooler temperatures before shipping. Plugs are nonflowering plants and will immediately be placed in a greenhouse, which makes them easier to ship without losing quality.

Holding and storing plants

Plugs. Research has demonstrated that plugs may be placed in 40° to 45°F (4° to 7°C), preferably, but not necessarily, with light. Species listed in Group B (see temperature toning) should be stored at a warmer temperature (45° to 48°F) than those in Group A (40°F). Low light levels from incandescent or special cold fluorescent lamps are recommended in the cooler. Apply a fungicide prior to moving plugs into the cooler, water sparingly and do not fertilize. Plugs may be kept up to 3 weeks under these conditions. Remove from the cooler in the evening or very early morning and place under shade cloth. Moving plants immediately from the cooler to the greenhouse bench is like taking them from the Gulf of Alaska and plunging them into a steam room . . . not a good idea.

The above scenario falls apart when storing dense plug trays. The smaller the plug (512, 800), the fewer days it can remain useful if not transplanted. If you order plants in dense plugs, be prepared to transplant immediately.

Plants in flower. Sometimes plants must remain in the greenhouse an extra week or so because of poor weather, poor scheduling or poor sales. Not only does everything back up, but flowers begin to abscise and plants

decline. Horizontal discharge fans help immensely to cool the greenhouse as well as dispel pollutants such as ethylene. Cool the greenhouse down as much as possible, and reduce watering and fertility practices. If coolers are available, plants may be stored as previously mentioned (place plants in toning Group A or Group B). Lights are necessary for long-term storage (greater than 5 days), or flowers will fall off rapidly.

The grower can make a significant difference in bedding plant postproduction life. Each practice outlined in this chapter may not have much influence by itself, but together these practices may be integrated into a growing program to significantly improve bedding plant shelf life. A summary table below outlines beneficial grower practices starting from initial production until plants leave the greenhouse (Table 13).

Table 13
Ways to increase bedding plant shelf life

	Comments	Importance*
1. Beginning production		
Sowing time:	The later the sowing, the more stress on plants on the retail shelf. Late sowings should be planted in larger containers.	3
Container volume:	Final container should be as large as economically possible. This is particularly true for late sowings.	5
Medium:	If mix is well drained and well aerated so that a good crop can be produced, medium is of little importance.	2
	Adding soil (~10%) helps shelf life.	3
Hydrogel:	Adding hydrogel to the medium may be effective but research has indicated contradictory results.	3
2. During production period		
Growth regulators:	If grown in warm conditions without growth regulators, plants will be leggy and decline rapidly.	4
3. Toning practices		
Reducing temperature:	Reduce temperature by 5° to 8°F (3° to 5°C) when flower bud is visible.	4
Reducing fertility:	Reduce fertility concentration 50% when flower bud is visible.	5
Reducing water:	Reduce watering frequency when bud is visible. This goes hand-in-hand with fertility reduction.	5
4. Out the door:	Be sure all dead leaves and dead flowers are removed and plants are well watered.	5

* Rating: 5=very important; 1=unimportant.

Shipping environment

Since plants will be placed in a stressful situation, it's important to reduce as many additional potential problems as possible. A well-ventilated area for boxing and packing reduces ethylene gas around the plants. It's important not to add the gas itself from automobile exhaust or any other sources such as dead and dying tissue to the trailer or box. Don't allow any idling trucks or gas-powered forklifts in the area. If engines must be running, it's essential to ventilate. (See Table 14.)

Table 14
Ethylene in exhaust samples

		Ethylene (ppm)
Automobile	(new)	97
	(old)	160
	(very old)	210
Diesel vehicle		64

Source: Adapted from Haseko.

Keep in mind when looking at the above table that 0.1 ppm concentrations can be hazardous to plants and 10 ppm can cause death within hours. New, stringent emission standards adopted since these data were compiled have significantly decreased ethylene amounts; auto exhaust, however, is still a major ethylene producer.

The shipping area should also be kept cool—as close to 40°F (5°C) as workers can tolerate. Even 60°F (16°C) is better than 70°F (21°C). Ethylene production depends on concentration, length of exposure time and temperature. Cool temperatures will reduce the amount of ethylene produced as well as slow down plant metabolism.

Transportation environment

Shipping in the dark. Lack of light sets in motion processes that reduce plant quality. Respiration—a tearing-down process—continues unabated and speeds up if temperatures rise, and photosynthesis—a building process—shuts down in the dark. The balance shifts from tissue production in the well-lit greenhouse to tissue breakdown in darkness. The other grim reality of shipping in the dark, particularly over a long time (48 to 96 hours), is the resulting ethylene gas buildup. Stressing plants causes an increase in ethylene production and, if leaves are yellowing or disease organisms present, the additional stress can result in levels of 0.1 to 1.0 ppm ethylene surrounding the plants. It would be nice if trucks had racks with fluorescent tubes, but they don't.

Species differ in their response to darkness. Nearly all stretch to varying degrees, and leaves of some species become rapidly chlorotic. Generally less than 48 hours in the dark won't be detrimental; however, longer periods of time in warm, dark trucks can be quite harmful (Table 15).

Table 15
Effect of total darkness on bedding plants

	Height increase (%)			
	2 days	5 days	7 days	Comments (after 7 days)
Ageratum Madison	2	13	14	Stretches at upper internodes. Flowers small, some chlorosis.
Begonia Scarlanda	2	4	5	Little stretch, leaves chlorotic and rotting.
Celosia Century Mix	2	14	15	Little damage, leaves look excellent.
Dianthus White	5	7	8	Little stretch but flowers not opening.
Eggplant T & M Mix	13	21	28	Significant stretch, leaves and flowers abscising, flowers abscising, significant leaf chlorosis.
Impatiens Accent Red	5	10	12	Flowers abscising.
Marigold Janie Mix	6	9	11	Small flowers, small leaves.
Petunia Resisto Rose	6	25	37	Small flowers, faded small leaves.
Pentas Egyptian Star	8	12	13	Flowers fade, leaves chlorotic.

Bedding Plants Postproduction Factors

The above research was conducted at temperatures between 70° and 80°F (21° and 27°C). If temperatures were much warmer, damage would be more rapid; if temperatures were cooler, less effects from darkness would be seen.

Shipping containers. One of the greatest problems in shipping plants is the lack of light and ventilation in the trailer or shipping container. Because of economics, flats may be stacked up, often resulting in poor air movement. Plugs and started plants are often shipped in boxes without any ventilation. The ride may be short, but the stress is high.

When plants are placed in nonventilated boxes, ethylene levels can rise very high. Research on geranium plantlets in nonventilated containers showed ethylene increased tenfold or more with a concomitant rise in chlorotic leaves even when temperatures were lowered (Table 16).

Table 16
Nonvented boxes affect plant quality during shipping

Temperature	Number of yellow leaves after 48 hours		Ethylene concentration (nl/l)	
	Vented	Nonvented	Vented	Nonvented
At 78° to 92°F (no cooling)	3	5	7	100
Precooled to 50°F and shipped at 50°F	$1\frac{1}{2}$	$1\frac{1}{2}$	15	68

Source: Adapted from Dean.

The number of yellow leaves doesn't seem very high, but when you think that only about eight to 10 yellow leaves were present before shipping, the numbers take on more meaning. If chlorotic leaves and abscised buds are a problem when shipping in nonvented boxes, you might try a new box design.

Temperature. The single most important environmental factor in maintaining plant quality is temperature. Keeping plants cool slows down plant metabolism, reducing respiration and net loss of dry weight during shipping. Cool temperatures also make plants less sensitive to any ethylene present.

Research has shown that young plants lose more chlorophyll when subjected to 1 ppm ethylene as temperature increases.

When no ethylene is present, chlorophyll loss is less severe, even if temperatures become warmer. When temperatures are warm compared to cool, the presence of ethylene in a dark, warm, unventilated environment, such as a truck trailer, causes plants to become highly chlorotic.

As shown in Table 10, all bedding plants should be shipped at either 50° to 55°F (10° to 13°C) (Group A) or 58° to 62°F (15° to 17°C) (Group B). A mixed crop of Group A and B species should be shipped at 55° to 60°F (13° to 16°C). Realistically, of course, this isn't always possible. Refrigerated trucks might be too expensive, unavailable or the distance too short for the additional expense. Although chemicals exist that can inhibit respiration, ethylene synthesis or chlorophyll breakdown, they're experimental and may result in damage, or they aren't sufficiently effective for commercial application and are not recommended.

Plugs. When shipping seedlings or plugs, all the above practices hold true. Ethylene's effects can even be more insidious, however. For example, in geraniums, a shipping concentration of only 0.1 ppm ethylene for 2 to 3 days when plants were approximately 7 weeks old resulted in a 1-week delay in flowering. Although it seems likely that flowering of ethylene-sensitive plants (Table 20) would also be delayed, this hasn't been tested with other bedding plant species.

There's no panacea for plant transportation problems, but it should be possible to provide ventilation in the trailer, use a ventilated shipping box perhaps, provide some incandescent lighting and, at the very least, schedule some of the journey during cooler morning or evening temperatures. As with grower responsibilities, each of these practices alone is of little value, but together, they can significantly improve the plant's shelf life once it has left the greenhouse. Table 17 gives a summary of practices to improve quality during the shipping and transportation stage of bedding plant production.

Table 17
Increasing bedding plants' shelf life during shipping and transportation

Practice	Comments	Importance*
Shipping area		
No gasoline combustion engines	Engines emit large amounts of ethylene; use electric engines if necessary in shipping area.	5
Keep cool	Cool temperatures reduce ethylene sensitivity.	3
Keep well ventilated	Air movement reduces any ethylene buildup.	4
In the truck		
Handle plants gently	Rough handling breaks stems, leaves and flowers and promotes ethylene gas.	4
Keep truck cool (55° to 60°F)	Cooling reduces ethylene buildup and reduces plant metabolism. Travel in early morning or evening to take advantage of naturally cooler temperatures.	5

* 5=very important; 1=unimportant

Retail area: *The retail management's responsibility*

The retail area is many things to many people. Some people think of a retail area as an extension of their greenhouse—a well-lit, well-ventilated polyethylene or glass structure. Others see plants placed helter-skelter on a sunbaked sidewalk, lying wounded from consumers' inquisitive hands.

The best environment for displaying and holding bedding plants is a climate-controlled display greenhouse. Here plants may be handled without damage, cool but comfortable temperatures can be maintained and light and water can be carefully controlled. Unfortunately, this is seldom the case, and marketers are presently selling large volumes of bedding plants in areas that are seldom designed for bedding plant displays. When personnel from a large chain store with heavy spring bedding plant sales recently gathered, they commented that because plant losses were so bad, management was seriously considering disbanding their whole garden program. This is a situation the entire industry must face. If one segment of our market is lost, no matter how big or how small, everyone suffers. We cannot stand by and watch a store or chain of stores make plant handling mistakes that will eventually lead to their abandoning plant sales. It's the responsibility of growers, distributors and educators to provide information to those selling our product.

The retailer, however, has a responsibility to provide an environment that prolongs the product's life and to display and market the plants so consumers will want to buy them. The retailer has many important roles. The most important are:

Buy good quality plants

Retailers who pay a few more cents per flat for better quality are repaid in two crucial ways. First, higher quality material sells more rapidly. This accelerates turnover and reduces shelf life problems. And, second, higher quality material lasts longer on the shelf. The old adage of "junk in equals junk out" is particularly appropriate in this case. Plants already subjected to undue stress on the production bench are less able to cope with greater stress on the retail shelf. The retailer who deals with growers incorporating a postproduction phase into their production program has fewer shelf life problems. Benefits to the grower become more obvious as retailers understand the role growers play in their product's shelf life. A grower should be able to market his crop more aggressively and ask top dollar when he incorporates a postproduction program into his operation.

Personnel

I visited a fast food restaurant one day around 2 p.m. when few customers were present. The tables were clean, the food handled in an orderly fashion, and the place was spotless. I went back 2 days later during the busy lunch hour, and the tables were messy, French fries decorated the floor, and food was being handled sloppily. The place was a mess! This situation is similar to a garden center or mass market outlet. In the spring when it's busy, there seldom are enough knowledgeable salespeople. Nothing turns people away faster than poor-looking plants and a messy area. So it's important to provide some training to temporary helpers. At the very least, they should know:

(1) Plants shouldn't be watered without water breakers. This sounds so simple, yet, in many outlets a hose is unavailable, let alone a hose breaker. Knocking over plants by using the "firehose" technique of watering results in ethylene production and very poor shelf life.

(2) Keep plants and surrounding areas clean. There must be enough people, even during the busiest times, to clean up. Removing dead and injured plants, spent flowers and general carnage is essential at least twice a day during the busy season. Not only do people get turned off when plants are dangling from their roots, but high ethylene concentrations can be produced. A skilled employee isn't necessary for these jobs, but a competent one certainly is.

Regardless of the type of retail outlet where plants are sold, at least one worker should know how to water properly and keep plants groomed. Often, even this minimum standard care is sorely lacking. The saying that "the store only sells water hoses, but never uses them" needs to disappear from industry's language.

Shading

Plants stocked at retail outlets should be shaded from the sun regardless of species, especially when 68°F (20°C) or higher temperatures are expected (Table 18).

Table 18
Light intensity affects petunia postproduction life[*]

Temperature	Days held at low light	Days held at medium light	Days held at high light
86°F	12	11	5
68°F	12	13	7

Adapted from Armitage and Kowalski (1983a).

These data show that light (no shading) reduces postproduction life even with moderate temperatures (68°F; 20°C). Usually, areas with no shade are considerably warmer. Shading can be provided with shade cloth, fiberglass panels or canvas cloth. Plants may even be arranged under shade trees. Full sunlight on a bright day at 2 p.m. is about 8,000 fc (86.1 klux). Recent research by Nelson showed that for most bedding plants, optimal light levels in the retail area should be between 250 to 700 fc (2.7 to 7.5 klux); this translates into significant shade. Since not all days are equally cloudless, and since full sun occurs only between 12:00 and 3:00 p.m., 50% to 60% shade material is enough to reduce sunlight to appropriate levels. This is especially true as the season progresses and light intensity increases. If afternoon temperatures aren't expected to rise above 65°F (18°C), then the value of shade is minimized. It's encouraging to see larger volume retailers raising plants off the sidewalk and putting them under well-ventilated, heavily shaded areas for bedding plant sales.

Unfortunately, the shading concept can be taken too far. One particular outlet had approximately 70% shade but was still displaying the flats on tiers of shelves. Plants on all but the highest tier were receiving little enough light at the best of times; adding a shade structure was like locking them in the cupboard. Species such as alyssum, coleus and tomato do poorly with such low light and are the first to decline. There's no worse place to keep bedding plants than on tiered shelves where they receive too little light, too little ventilation and suffer too much damage.

Ventilation

Good air movement is essential in the retail area. Lack of ventilation due to surrounding buildings, fences, traffic or parked cars must be avoided for two obvious reasons: pollution and temperature. Air movement naturally dilutes pollutant buildup, and it also reduces temperature. If plants are subjected to ethylene from damaged tissue or automobiles, air movement will reduce the concentration and reduce the damage. Auto traffic is unavoidable in and near many retail locations, and pollutants can rise to dangerous concentrations. Air samples taken from retail outlets during April and May yielded values as high as 0.5 ppm ethylene, which if prolonged, result in plant damage. Some plant species, as well as certain plant parts, are more susceptible to ethylene damage than others. Table 19 shows that members of the Compositae family (marigolds or zinnias) are little affected by ethylene, whereas impatiens are susceptible. It's also interesting to note that mature flower buds are much more prone to falling off than young flowers or leaves.

Table 19
**Various bedding plants'
ethylene sensitivity**

	Flower abscission (%) when exposed to 1 ppm ethylene		
	No exposure	3 hours	6 hours
Impatiens	3	71	98
Salvia	2	20	50
Zinnia	0	0	0

Although there isn't enough research to determine all bedding plants' ethylene sensitivity, the following table may be useful.

Table 20
**Various bedding plants'
ethylene sensitivity***

Insensitive	Moderate	High
Alyssum	Begonia	Geranium (petal shatter)
Calendula	Coleus	Impatiens
Marigold	Petunia	Salvia
Ornamental pepper		Snapdragon
Zinnia		

Based on exposure of 1 ppm for 3, 6, 12, 24 or 48 hours.

In practical terms, little can be done about automobile traffic except to display less susceptible species, such as zinnia or other composites, nearer the road and place those more susceptible, such as impatiens, as far from contamination as possible. Building a display area that doesn't restrict air flow also helps reduce the ethylene problem. Even more important, air flow also helps reduce temperature. Combined with shading, it helps keep temperature within safe limits. It's easy to increase ventilation and air movement by using overhead fans in the greenhouse or retail area.

Temperature

Temperature is the most important factor to control in the retail area, as well as the greenhouse and shipping area. If temperatures are maintained near 50°F (10°C), then light intensity, fertilizer, shade and ventilation are of little importance. Most experiments with bedding plants show that cool temperatures are the most important environmental factor in increasing shelf life. In experiments where different production practices such as high or low irrigation frequencies, different fertilizer regimens or different greenhouse temperatures were used, plants held at 50°F (10°C), unlike those in warmer retail areas, showed few differences due to production or shipping treatments. Although most plants such as petunias, geraniums and marigolds persist longer at cool temperatures, others like impatiens prefer warmer temperatures near 60°F (16°C); only coleus performed best above 70°F (21°C). Regardless of whether the optimum temperature is 50° or 60°F (10° or 16°C), obvious practical problems abound.

Keeping temperatures at 50° to 60°F is pleasant for the plants, but it's not terribly pleasant for people. It's also impractical during spring and almost impossible during the summer. Today's consumer is much more interested in his drink being chilled at 40°F (5°C) than his bedding plants being stored at 55°F (13°C). Until we accept the fact that plants must be placed at cool temperatures to ensure maximum shelf life, warm temperatures in the retail area will always be a problem. Shading and air movement help greatly in keeping temperatures cooler and are, along with good grooming and housecleaning, the best means to ensure high quality plants on the retail shelf. Retailers can help maintain fresh-looking plants by providing competent personnel, care and the proper environment. The greatest problems in the postproduction chain occur in the retail area. Fortunately, these are easily solved. Unfortunately, they won't be solved until growers and retail management cooperate to provide sound postproduction practices. Table 21 summarizes retail practices that improve bedding plant quality in the retail environment.

Table 21
Beneficial retail practices

Practice	Comments	Importance*
Buy from a grower with an integrated post-production program.	Plants pretreated for post-production enrichment will have additional shelf life.	4
Personnel	Have enough staff to water properly and to clean up area.	4
Grooming plants	Grooming is essential to reduce ethylene sources and to make plants more attractive so that they sell more quickly.	5
Shading	Providing 50% to 60% shade will reduce temperature and water loss.	4
Ventilation	Good air movement dilutes ethylene and other contaminants; it also helps to reduce temperature.	3
Temperature	Use shading and ventilation where possible to reduce temperature.	5

* 5=very important; 1=unimportant

Garden area: *The consumer's responsibility*

A bedding plant's ultimate destination is a garden setting, whether it be six petunias in an apartment planter or 600 for a condominium complex entrance. The consumer is responsible for the plants' garden performance. Consumers form two primary groups: the commercial buyer and the home gardener. Commercial buyers include landscape contractors who plant in large numbers. They deal directly with the grower and, by eliminating the retail outlet, they also eliminate some postproduction problems. Nevertheless, plants produced by a grower with an integrated postproduction program are much preferred to those produced without such a program.

Good soil preparation and proper site selection are essential. Few plants, no matter how well grown or how well tended in transport, will grow successfully in beds with poor drainage and infertile soil. Similarly, impatiens can't be expected to thrive in full sun nor geraniums in heavy shade. Proper sites for many annuals appear in Table 22.

Selecting cultivars suited for particular environments is of basic importance. Some cultivars are more heat tolerant, and they grow better in the South than the North and vice versa. Visiting trial grounds near the job site is the best way for landscapers to evaluate garden performance of potentially useful cultivars. Not to take the time to do so is foolish.

The second and historically most important consumer group is the home gardener. He or she may buy a dozen begonias or one geranium and has absolutely no knowledge or interest in why, where or how the plants were grown or handled. The gardener is the first to reject a dirty, ill-managed retail outlet that sells poor quality. Although some say that people buy simply for price, surveys show otherwise. The home gardener's responsibility, then, is to consider plants based on quality before price. Well-grown plants, shipped properly, and held in retail areas where each step preserves quality for the consumer, may be slightly more expensive but well worth the price. Home gardeners should buy from retailers who obviously take pride in their plants, not from an outlet

Table 22
Site selection for planting annuals outdoors

Botanic name	Common name
Varieties for shade or semishade locations	
Antirrhinum majus	Snapdragon
Begonia semperflorens	Begonia
Calendula officinalis	Calendula
Campanula sp.	Bellflower
Centaurea moschata	Sweet sultan
Cheiranthus cheiri	Wallflower
Clarkia elegans	Clarkia
Coleus blumei	Coleus
Consolida	Morning Glory
Coreopsis tinctoria	Calliopsis
Delphinium ajacis	Larkspur
Godetia grandiflora	Godetia
Impatiens sp.	Impatiens
Lobelia erinus	Dwarf lobelia
Lobularia marltima	Sweet alyssum
Mirabilis jalapa	Four o'clock
Myosotis scorpioides	Forget-me-not
Nicotiana alata	Flowering tobacco
Phlox drummondii	Annual phlox
Rudbeckia hirta	Rudbeckia
Salvia splendens	Scarlet sage
Salvia farinacea	Mealy-cup sage
Torenia fournieri	Wishbone plant
Tropaeolum majus	Nasturtium
Verbena hybrida	Verbena
Viola sp.	Pansy

Botanic name	Common name
Varieties for dry locations	
Ageratum houstonianum	Ageratum
Brachycome iberidifolia	Swan River daisy
Celosia argentea	Cockscomb
Cleome spinosa	Spider flower
Coreopsis tinctoria	Calliopsis
Cosmos bipinnatus	Cosmos
Dimorphotheca sp.	Cape marigold
Eschscholzia californica	California poppy
Lampranthus emarginatus	Ice plant
Limonium sp.	Statice
Mesembryanthemum sp.	Ice plant
Mirabilis jalapa	Four o'clock
Petunia hybrida	Petunia
Portulaca grandiflora	Moss rose
Verbena hybrida	Verbena
Zinnia sp.	Zinnia
Varieties for moist locations	
Datura suaveolens	Angel trumpet
Hibiscus sp.	Hibiscus
Lathyrus odoratus	Sweet pea
Myosotis scorpioides	Forget-me-not
Varieties for poor soil	
Celosia argentea	Celosia
Clarkia elegans	Clarkia
Cosmos bipinnatus	Cosmos
Eschscholzia californica	California poppy
Euphorbia marginata	Snow-on-the-mountain

where, if plants are not sold immediately off the truck, they decline in 2 days. Home gardeners have the same responsibilities as landscape contractors regarding bed preparation and site selection.

The consumer may be the last link in the postproduction chain but is just as important as the other links. It's a shame when the consumer, for whom plants have been produced, shipped, stored and handled, destroys all that effort by improper selection and care of those same plants.

Table 23 provides some consumer responsibilities that prolong bedding plant life.

Table 23
How consumers can increase bedding plant life

Practice	Comments	Importance*
Landscape contractor		
Purchase plants from grower with an an integrated post-production program.	Plants will transplant better and establish faster.	3
Select proper cultivars based on observations at field trials.	Cultivars intolerant of local conditions will do poorly regardless of how maintained.	5
Home consumer		
Purchase plants from retail outlet that has good postproduction practices that maintain health and vigor.	Plants will transplant better and establish faster.	4
All users		
Prepare bed well by incorporating organic matter, checking pH and improving drainage.	Plants can't do well in heavy clay or light sand soils—they'll languish and die.	5
Select suitable species for garden site.	Sun-loving plants shouldn't be planted in shade and vice versa.	5

* 5=very important; 1=unimportant

These practices help establish plants in their final setting and give them an excellent start toward attaining their full potential beauty. Once plants are properly sited and placed in good soil, postproduction practices become less significant and maintenance procedures, such as removing spent flowers, fertilizing and supporting the plants, become most important.

Conclusion

Postproduction losses of garden plants have been ignored far too long. Significant increases in shelf life can be attained but only if all aspects of the industry work together. Breeders, growers, truckers, shippers, retailers, wholesalers and consumers each have an opportunity and a responsibility to improve plant shelf life. One group can make a difference, but not until everyone makes a commitment to do their share will significant gains in postproduction life be realized. Our industry is alive and well: Let's join together to keep all its components healthy.

ADDITIONAL READING

Armitage, A.M., R. Heins, S. Dean and W. Carlson. 1980. Factors influencing petal flower abscission in the seed-propagated geranium. *Journal of the American Society of Horticultural Science* 105(9):562-564.

Armitage, A.M. 1982. Keeping quality of bedding plants—Whose responsibility is it? *Florists' Review* 171(4438):34-35, 39.

Armitage, A.M. and T. Kowalski. 1983a. Effects of light intensity and air temperature in simulated postproduction environment on *Petunia hybrida* Vilm. *Journal of the American Society of Horticultural Science* 108(1):115-118.

———. 1983b. Effect of irrigation frequency during greenhouse production on the postproduction quality of *Petunia hybrida* Vilm. *Journal of the American Society of Horticultural Science* 108(11):118-121.

Armitage, A.M., H.M. Vines, Z.P. Tu and C.C. Black. 1983. Water relations and net photosynthesis in hybrid geranium. *Journal of the American Society of Horticultural Science* 108(2):310-314.

Armitage, A.M. 1984. Gone and forgotten. *Greenhouse Grower* 2(5):36-37.

———. 1985. Will plug performance dictate industry directions? *Greenhouse Grower* 4(10):30, 32.

———. 1986a. Influence of production practices on postproduction life of bedding plants. *Acta Horticultura* 181:269-277.

———. 1986b. Chlormequat-induced early flowering of hybrid geranium. The influence of gibberellic acid. *HortScience* 21(1):116-118.

———. 1987. Work in progress.

Ball, V. 1991. *Ball RedBook*. Geneva, IL: Ball Publishing.

Bearce, B.C. and R.W. McCollum. 1977. A comparison of peat-lite and noncomposted hardwood bark mixes for use in pot and bedding plant production and the effects of a new hydrogel soil amendment on their performance. *Florists' Review* Oct. 27:21-23, 66.

Boodley, J.W., J. Kumpf and B. Pollinger. 1983. An evaluation of soil vs. peat-lite media on postproduction life of selected potted chrysanthemums. *Connecticut Greenhouse Newsletter* 117:11-12.

Connecticut Greenhouse Crop Production Task Force. 1983. *Connecticut Greenhouse Newsletter* 117:11.

Conover, C.A. 1977. Effects of acclimatization. *Proceedings of the Environmental Conditioning Symposium* Washington, DC: Hort. Research Institute.

——— and R.T. Poole. 1979. Influence of pH on activity of Viterra 2 and effects on growth of Maranta and Pilea. *Proceedings of the Florida State Horticultural Society* 332-333.

Dean, M.S. 1979. "A study of simulated environmental shipping conditions on senescence and transplant recovery of seedling geranium (*Pelargonium x hortorum* Bailey)." M.S. thesis, Michigan State University.

Eikhof, R.H., P.A. King and G.H. Koven. 1974. Control of wilting in potted plants. *Ohio Florists' Association Bulletin* 532.

Fonteno, W.C. and E.L. McWilliams. 1978. Light compensation and acclimatization of four tropical foliage plants. *Journal of the American Society of Horticultural Science* 103(1):52-56.

Gehring, T.M. and A.J. Lewis. 1979a. Extending the shelf life of bedding plants. I. Container volume. *Florists' Review* 165(4278):17, 60-61.

———. 1979b. Extending the shelf life of bedding plants. II. Hydrogel. *Florists' Review* 165(4282):30, 46.

Gehring, T.M. and A.J. Lewis. 1980. Extending the shelf life of bedding plants. III. Antitranspirants. *Florists' Review* 165(4286):31, 65.

Gehring, T.M. 1979c. "Shelf life extension of bedding plants." M.S. thesis, Virginia Polytech. Institute.

Hardenburg, R.E., A.E. Watada and L.Y. Wang. 1986. The commercial storage of fruits, vegetables and florist and nursery stocks. *USDA Agricultural Handbook* 66:136.

Hasek, R.F., H.A. James and R.H. Siaroni. 1969. Ethylene—its effect on flower crops II. *Florists' Review* 144(3722):16-17, 53-55.

James, E.A. and D. Richards. 1986. The influence of iron source on the water-holding properties of potting media amended with water-absorbing polymers. *Scientia Horticultura* 28:201-208.

Johnson, M.S. 1984. Effect of soluble salts on water absorption by gel-forming soil conditions. *Journal of Science, Food and Agriculture* 35:1063-1066.

Kaczperski, M. and A.M. Armitage. 1990. Short-term storage of plug-grown bedding plant seedlings. *HortScience* 25:1094.

Koranski, D., P. Karlovich and A. Al-Hemaid. 1989. The latest research on holding and shipping plugs. *GrowerTalks* 53(8):72, 74, 76, 78-79.

Lange, N.E. and R.D. Heins. 1991. Cold storage of bedding plant plugs. *HortScience* 26 (Abst. 618):153-154.

Lewis, A.J. 1979. Antitranspirant effect on water ions from hydrangea. *HortScience* 14(2):131 (Abstr).

Marousky, F.T. and B.K. Harbaugh. 1981. Influence of temperature, light and ethylene on seedlings of geranium (*Pelargonium x hortorum*) during simulated shipping conditions. *Journal of the American Society of Horticultural Science* 106(5):527-530.

Masterlerz, J.J. 1986. *Bedding Plants III*. University Park, PA: Pennsylvania Flower Growers,

Nell, T.A. and J.E. Barrett. 1986. Production light level effects on light compensation point, carbon exchange rate and postproduction longevity of poinsettia. *Acta Horticultura* 181:257-262.

Nelson, L.J., A.M. Armitage and W.H. Carlson. 1980. Keeping quality of marigolds and impatiens as affected by night temperature and duration. *Florists' Review* 167(4318):28-29, 62, 74.

Nelson, L. and W. Carlson. 1987. Improve the marketability of bedding plants. *Greenhouse Grower* 5(3):84-85.

Nelson, L.J. 1984. "The influence of environmental factors on postproduction keeping quality of bedding plants." M.S. thesis, Michigan State University.

Post, K. 1955. *Florist crop production and marketing.* New York: Orange Judd Publishing Co.

Reid, M.S. 1985. Ethylene in the care and handling of ornamentals. *Society of American Florists.* Florists June 22-23, 25.

Sanderson, K.C. 1978. Annuals for special uses. *BPI News,* May 4-7.

Spoomer, A. 1979. Container soils—who's mixing who? *Proceedings of the 12th BPI Conference,* Chicago 177-186.

Staby, G.L., J.C. Robertson, D.C. Kiplinger and C.A. Conover. 1978. *Chain of Life*, Ohio Florists Association.

Staby, G.L. 1986. Bedding plant life after production: insufficient questions, answers. *Floral and Nursery Times* 26 (Sept.):26-27.

Still, S. 1976. Growth of Sunny Mandalay chrysanthemums in hardwood bark-amended media as affected by insolubilized poly(ethylene oxide). *HortScience* 11:483-484.

Tayama, H.K., R.K. Lindquist, C.C. Powell, V. Zrebiec, J.D. Holden, D.S. Koranski, R.J. Precheur and J. Selley. 1987. *Tips on Growing Bedding Plants.* Ohio State University.

Tu, Z.P., A.M. Armitage and H.M. Vines. 1985. Influence of an antitranspirant and a hydrogel on net photosynthesis and water loss of cineraria during water stress. *HortScience* 20(3):386-388.

United States Department of Agriculture, 1991. *Floriculture crops, 1990 summary.*

Vlahos, J. and J.W. Boodley. 1973. Hydrogel and its potential use. *Florists' Review* 152(3929):21-22.

Voigt, A.O. 1991. Sales were strong for the 1990 bedding plant season, despite adverse weather conditions. *PPGA Newsletter* 22:Special Report.

Wise, F.C. 1980. "Growth regulator studies of factors affecting postproduction performance and quality of petunias." M.S. thesis, North Carolina State University.

Crop-by-crop postproduction care and handling

The next section lists some of the more important bedding plant species and describes how to enhance their postproduction performance. *The Postproduction Factors section is a prerequisite to this crop-by-crop section.* Although species are treated separately here, use the material from the Postproduction Factors section to fill in any information gaps. Because little research has been conducted on individual crops, information is scarce, and the following list is incomplete.

CROPS

Ageratum

Family Name: **Asteraceae**
Common Name: **Flossflower**

A

A genus of approximately 30 species of annuals, subshrubs and shrubs. Only *A. houstonianum,* native to Central America, is commercially important.

AGERATUM

Production factors

Light. Low light levels will result in longer internodes and leaf abscission.

Temperature. Reduce night temperatures to 50° to 55°F (10° to 13°C) at visible bud. Ageratum is tender, and temperatures below 40°F (4°C) cause injury and reduce postproduction life.

Nutrition. Reducing nitrogen by half at visible bud stage and continuing until flowers open increases longevity. Do not stop fertilizing completely.

Container. Plants should be grown in as large a container as possible. The most economical method is to increase container depth. In experiments, plants grown in 4-inch (10 cm) deep pots lasted 26% longer than plants grown in 2-inch (5 cm) deep pots. Plants in 4-inch pots have greater longevity than those grown in cell packs due to greater water retention.

Soil amendments. Various reports conflict on the use of hydrophilic polymers (Hydrogel, Viterra) for extending shelf life. Research with plants grown in 2x2x2-inch (5x5x5-cm) pots showed that ageratum did not wilt as quickly with hydrogel incorporated into the medium, so it may be a useful amendment.

Postproduction factors

Shipping, handling and storage

Temperature. Temperatures of 60° to 70°F (16° to 21°C) don't seriously affect quality if plants are transported or stored for only a short period of time. Temperatures of 50° to 55°F (10° to 13°C), however, are

A

preferred to reduce metabolism and plant stretch. Avoid temperatures below 45°F (7°C).

Gases. Moderately sensitive to ethylene.

Seedling storage. Although not recommended, seedlings may be stored up to 2 weeks. When seedlings have reached the proper transplanting stage, water containers thoroughly. After excess water has drained, place containers in polyethylene bags, and seal the bags with rubber bands. Store them in a 35° to 40°F (2° to 4°C) refrigerator, 12 inches below fluorescent lamps. Keep lights on 14 hours daily.

Retail handling

Light. Keep plants out of full sun to reduce drying out of the soil. Shade 50% to 60% in spring. Required degree of shade depends on the outlet's latitude and elevation. More shade is needed farther south and in summer.

Temperature. If selling outside, reduce the temperature with shade and ventilation. If selling from a greenhouse, cool to 60° to 65°F (16° to 18°C) if possible.

Irrigation. Water plants in the morning before opening the store. Don't water later than 5 p.m. unless absolutely necessary.

Grooming. Retail areas attract high consumer traffic; it's essential to dispose of broken stems, spent flowers and any dead or decaying tissue to reduce ethylene.

Consumer care

Planting. Break up all plants' root balls immediately upon planting.

Location. Plant in full sun in the Northern United States but in partial shade in the Southern states.

Grooming. For less disease problems and more frequent bloom, remove all spent flower heads.

Pests. Highly susceptible to whiteflies.

ADDITIONAL READING

Brodley, J.W., A. Bing, T.C. Wesler, L. Albright, M. Daughtrey, M. Semel and M. Topoleshi. 1984. Storage of seedlings. *Cornell Bedding Plant Guidelines for New York State.* 1984:5.

Gehring, T.M. and A.J. Lewis. 1979. Extending the shelf life of bedding plants: A. Hydrogel. *Florists' Review* 165(4282):30, 46.

Gehring, J.M. 1979. "Shelf life extension of bedding plants." M.S. thesis, Virginia Polytechnic Institute.

———. 1979. Extending the shelf life of bedding plants, I. Container volume. *Florists' Review* 165(4278):17, 60-61.

Krone, P.R. 1937. The reaction of greenhouse plants to gas in the atmosphere and soil. *Michigan State University Experimental Station Special Bulletin* 285:1-35.

Tayama, H.K., R.K. Lindquist, C.C. Powell, V. Zebiec, H.D. Holden, D.S. Koranski, R.J. Precheur and J.G. Seeley. 1987. *Tips on Growing Bedding Plants.* Columbus: Ohio State University

Zimmerman, P.W. 1930. The response of plants to illuminating gas. *Proc. Amer. Soc. Hort. Sci.* 27:53-56.

Antirrhinum

an-ti-*ry*-num

Family Name: **Scrophulariaceae**
Common Name: **Snapdragon**

A genus of approximately 40 species. Mostly perennial, but usually grown as annuals. Only *A. majus*, the common snapdragon, is commercially important.

SNAPDRAGON

Production factors

Light. Low light levels will result in poor foliar color, longer internodes and sparse flowering.

Temperature. Snapdragons are cool temperature plants; temperatures above 70°F (21°C) result in internode elongation, reducing market life.

Nutrition. Reducing fertilizer when spike starts to elongate will likely help postproduction life.

Soil amendments. A well-drained, moisture-retaining medium is most beneficial for extending shelf life.

Postproduction factors

Shipping, handling and storage

Light. Plants held up to 4 days in the dark at 70°F (21°C) tend to stretch and flowers fade.

Temperature. Cool temperatures 50° to 55°F (10° to 13°C) are best for snapdragons, both in trucks and in holding greenhouses.

Gases. Very sensitive to ethylene.

Seedling storage. Although not recommended, seedlings may be stored up to 2 weeks. When seedlings have reached the proper transplanting stage, water containers thoroughly. After excess water has drained, place containers in polyethylene bags, and seal the bags with rubber bands. Store them in a 35° to 40°F (2° to 4°C) refrigerator, 12 inches below fluorescent lamps. Keep lights on 14 hours daily. Snapdragon seedlings can be stored this way for 4 to 6 weeks.

Antirrhinum

Retail handling

Light. Keep plants out of full sun to reduce water loss. Shade 50% to 60% in spring, depending on latitude and elevation.

Temperature. Reducing the temperature with ventilation and shade is beneficial to postproduction life.

Irrigation. Snapdragons require a good deal of water and must be irrigated often. They're more tolerant of stress than impatiens or petunias, however. Water early in the morning before temperatures warm up.

Grooming. Flowers tend to fall off and the decaying tissue releases ethylene. Remove spent blooms to help minimize ethylene levels.

Marketing. In the South, sell snapdragons in the fall for spring bloom, along with pansies. The cooler selling season also simplifies retail handling.

Consumer care

Planting. Break up root ball prior to planting in ground.

Location. A sunny location in the North, partial shade in the South. When mulched, plants will grow on as perennials in most of the United States.

Maintenance. Remove faded flower spikes to reduce disease.

ADDITIONAL READING

Adams, D.G. and W.A. Urdahl. 1972. Snapdragon stem breakage as related to stem lignification and flower color. *Journal of the American Society of Horticultural Science* 97:474-477.

Boodley, J.W., A. Bing, T.C. Weiler, L. Albright, M. Daughtrey, M. Semel and L. Topoleski. 1984. Storage of seedlings. *Cornell Bedding Plant Guidelines for NY State* 1984:5.

Cathey, H.M. and H.E. Heggestad. 1982. Ozone sensitivity of herbaceous plants: Modification by ethylenediurea. *J. Soc. Hort. Sci.* 107(6):1035-1042.

Dimock, A.W. and K.F. Baker. 1950. Ethylene produced by diseased tissue injures cut flowers. *Florists' Review* 106:27-29.

Flint, H.L. and S. Asen. 1953. The effects of various nutrient intensities on growth and development of snapdragons (*Antirrhinum majus* L.). *Proc. Amer. Soc. Hort. Sci.* 62:481-486.

Haney, W.J. 1959. Snapdragons that are shatter resistant. *National Snapdragon Society Bulletin* 10:5.

Mastalerz, J.W. 1952. Nitrate levels, light intensity, growing temperatures and keeping qualities of flowers held at 31°F. *N.Y. State Flower Grow. Bul.* 88:2-3.

Olson, N.L. and H.F. Wilkins. 1984. STS can improve cut flower and potted plant quality. *Minnesota State Florists Bulletin* 33(2):7-8.

A

36

Bedding Plants *Antirrhinum*

Begonia

bi-*gon*-ee-a

Family Name: **Begoniaceae**
Common Name: **Wax Begonia**

A huge genus of over 1,000 species from the tropics and subtropics of both hemispheres. Hybridization has given rise to over 10,000 recorded hybrids. Only *Begonia semperflorens* x *cultorum* hybrids—fibrous-rooted begonia—is the most commercially important.

PRELUDE BICOLOR

Production factors

Light. Grow begonias in full sun in winter. Although it's a shade-tolerant plant outdoors, low light levels in the greenhouse result in extended stretch and reduced shelf life.

Temperature. Temperatures within normal greenhouse range do not affect begonia shelf life.

Nutrition. High nitrogen fertility, particularly combined with low light, results in "soft" plants. Reducing nitrogen prior to finishing helps harden plants.

Postproduction factors

Shipping and handling

Light. Begonias are one of the first plants to stretch. Foliage of most cultivars becomes chlorotic and flowers fall off when placed in the dark. Shipping or storage more than 2 days in the dark results in lost shelf life.

Temperature. Avoid prolonged temperatures below 50°F (10°C), although begonias can tolerate temperatures in the low 40s if sufficiently hardened off by the grower.

Gases. Moderately sensitive to ethylene. Although begonias are little affected by concentrations of 1 ppm, plant exposure to 5 to 10 ppm ethylene for 12 hours results in 100% abscission of open flowers. Only 25% to 30% of the flower buds fall off, however.

Retail handling

Light. Inside the retail store, provide as much light as possible. Provide plants displayed outdoors with 50% to 60% shade, particularly if marketed in cell packs. If sold in 4- to 6-inch (10- to 15-cm) containers, less shade is necessary.

Begonia

bi-*gon*-ee-a

Temperature. Shading the plants reduces temperatures. Begonias will not be adversely affected at temperatures between 50° to 80°F (10° to 27°C).

Irrigation. Water thoroughly twice a day if temperatures are warm, and once a day otherwise, especially if plants are in cell packs. Begonias are sensitive to over-watering; watering more than twice a day is necessary only if plants show signs of severe wilting and soil is dry to the touch.

Consumer care

Planting. Break up soil ball prior to planting.

Location. Begonias are tolerant of shade and often treated as shade plants. Begonias have been used in full sun in most parts of the country, however, and many cultivars do equally well in the sun. Grown in full sun, the plant is more compact with smaller leaves but still performs well.

Maintenance. Flowers of large-flowered cultivars should be removed when faded because they might cause Botrytis. Small-flowered cultivars are self-cleaning, and flowers tend to fall off naturally.

ADDITIONAL READING

Cathey, H.M. and H.E. Heggestad. 1982. Ozone sensitivity of herbaceous plants: Modification by ethylenediurea. *Journal of the American Society of Horticultural Science* 107(6):1035-1042.

Harbaugh, B.K., G.L. Wilfret and F.J. Marousky. 1977. Utilization of sealed polyethylene packages for potted plants handled through mass market outlets. *HortScience* 12(4):409.

Harbaugh, B.K. and W.E. Waters. 1979. Evaluation of flowering potted plants under simulated home conditions. *HortScience* 14(6):743-745.

Marousky, F.J. and B.K. Harbaugh. 1982. Responses of certain flowering and foliage plants to exogenous ethylene. *Proceedings of the Florida State Horticultural Society* 95:159-162.

Nelson, L. and W. Carlson. 1987. Improve the marketability of bedding plants. *Greenhouse Grower* 5(3):84-85.

Celosia

ce-*lo*-see-a

Family Name: **Amaranthaceae**
Common Name: **Cockscomb**

A genus of about 60 annual and perennial herbaceous species. The main species used in bedding plant production is *Celosia argentea*, which has two forms: The feathered cockscomb is var. *plumosa* and the convoluted form is var. *cristata*.

JEWEL BOX MIX

Production factors

Light. Low light results in stretched, poor quality plants with reduced shelf life.

Temperature. Normal greenhouse temperatures probably won't affect shelf life.

Nutrition. Celosias are heavy feeders (300 ppm nitrogen constant liquid feed), but reduce nitrogen concentration 50% 1 to 2 weeks prior to sale.

Postproduction factors

Shipping and handling

Light. Placing celosia in areas of low light results in chlorotic foliage; however, the flowers are little affected by low light. They may be stored in the dark with minimal effect for 4 days.

Temperature. Just as with the effects of low light, low temperatures affect celosia foliage long before the flowers. Avoid temperatures below 45°F (7°C).

Gases. Celosia appears to be moderately sensitive to ethylene, although research to date shows severe leaf curl with exposures of 5 ppm for 3 days. This is a greater concentration and a longer time than normally encountered in a postproduction system, unless plants are sleeved. Celosia is very sensitive to ozone injury, however. Ethylenediurea provides good protection.

Retail handling

Light. As stated above, the foliage is much more susceptible to stress than the flowers. With adequate light, flowers of some celosia cultivars have been shown to outlast some chrysanthemum cultivars under simulated home conditions. Inside the retail

C

store, provide as much light as possible. Outside, provide 50% to 60% shade, particularly if the plants are being marketed in cell packs. Plants sold in 4- and 6-inch (10- to 15-cm) containers can tolerate a little less shade (minimum 40%).

Temperature. Celosia looks best at temperatures below 80°F (27°C), and shelf life is not markedly affected when temperatures are between 55° to 75°F (13° to 24°C). Shading results in lower temperatures and is beneficial to shelf life.

Irrigation. Water plants as necessary to avoid wilting.

Consumer care

Planting. Break up soil ball in preparation for planting.

Location. Plant celosia in full sun in the North. It can tolerate partial afternoon shade in the South.

Fertilization. Give plants at least two applications of a complete fertilizer within 60 days of planting.

Maintenance. Flowers last a long time, but lateral branches bearing additional flowers will elongate more readily if the central flower is removed when it fades.

ADDITIONAL READING

Cathey, H.M. and H.E. Haggestad. 1982. Ozone sensitivity of herbaceous plants: Modification by ethylenediurea. *Journal of the American Society of Horticultural Science* 107(6):1035-1042.

Harbaugh, B.K. and W.E. Waters. 1979. Evaluation of flowering potted plants under simulated home conditions. *HortScience* 14(6):743-745.

Marousky, F.J. and B.K. Harbaugh. 1982. Responses of certain flowering and foliage plants to exogenous ethylene. *Proceedings of the Florida State Horticultural Society* 95:159-162.

Coleus

-lee-us

Family Name: **Lamiaceae**
Common Name: **Coleus**

C

A genus of about 150 species of perennial, annual and subshrubs. The only species used commercially is *Coleus blumei*, characterized by its varied and brilliantly colored leaves. Native to Java.

WIZARD MIX

Production factors

There is no information available on how production practices influence postproduction life except the following:

Soils. There is no difference in shelf life between plants grown in soil-based and those grown in peat-lite media.

Temperature. Since coleus is tropical in origin, reducing temperatures below 55°F (13°C) prior to shipping would likely be detrimental.

Postproduction factors

Shipping and handling

No information except the following:

Gases. Coleus is moderately insensitive to ethylene. Leaves don't drop until 1 ppm has been present for approximately 24 hours.

Retail handling

Light. A minimum light intensity of 700 fc (7.5 klux) is necessary for optimum shelf life. This may be provided in a well-lit area or in a shaded greenhouse display area. If plants are displayed outside, 60% shade cloth or natural shade from pine trees, etc. will provide the proper light.

Temperature. In studies with various bedding plants, coleus was the only plant that had the best shelf life when placed at temperatures greater than 70°F (21°C). Since it can handle heat better than other species, it should survive a long shelf life.

Irrigation. Coleus leaves lose a great deal of water. Water at least twice a day to reduce wilting and subsequent loss of shelf life.

Coleus

ko-lee-us

Consumer care

Planting. Break up soil ball in preparation for planting.

Location. Plant in partial shade; there are no coleus cultivars that do well in full sun.

Maintenance. As coleus is grown mainly for the leaf color, the onset of flowering detracts from the foliage; remove flowers as they appear.

ADDITIONAL READING

Nelson. L.E. and W.H. Carlson. 1987. Improve the marketability of bedding plants. *Greenhouse Grower* 5(3):84-85.

Nelson, L.E. 1984. "The influence of environmental factors on postproduction keeping quality of bedding plants." M.S. thesis, Michigan State University.

C

Cosmos

kos-mos

Family Name: **Asteraceae**
Common Name: **Cosmos**

A genus of approximately 25 species. Historically, cosmos has been grown as a cut flower but recent breeding efforts have resulted in excellent garden cultivars. The two commercially important species are *Cosmos bipinnatus* and *C. sulphureus*. The latter is a better species for use as a bedding plant. Both cosmos species don't flower uniformly in a cell pack—they're better suited for 4-inch (10 cm) production or sold only as green plants in packs. Native to Mexico.

SONATA MIX

Production factors

Light. Low light results in poor foliar color, longer internodes and poor flowering.

Nutrition. High fertility is not recommended, particularly with *C. bipinnatus*. High nitrogen levels result in weak stems and poor shelf life.

Growth regulators. Using B-Nine to retard plant growth results in dwarf plants and some injury. Shelf life suffers accordingly.

Postproduction factors

Shipping, handling and storage

Light. Plants stretch if held in low light for more than 4 days.

Seedling storage. Although not recommended, seedlings may be stored up to 2 weeks. When seedlings have reached the proper transplanting stage, water containers thoroughly. After excess water has drained, place containers in polyethylene bags, and seal the bags with rubber bands. Store them in a 35° to 40°F (2° to 4°C) refrigerator, 12 inches (30 cm) below fluorescent lamps. Keep lights on 14 hours daily.

Retail handling

Light. If sold in cell packs outside, at least 50% shading is required.

Temperature. Reduce temperature through the use of ventilation and shade.

Irrigation. Water as needed; cosmos, however, is susceptible to leaf and root rot. Water in early morning and allow leaves to dry out to reduce chances for disease. Apply

Cosmos

the last irrigation early enough so plants don't sit in the evening air with wet foliage.

Consumer care

Planting. Break up soil ball in preparation for planting.

Location. Plant in full sun in well-prepared soil.

Maintenance. Deadhead plants to maintain vigor and reduce disease. If plants aren't deadheaded, they may die.

Dahlia

dal-ya

D

Family Name: **Asteraceae**
Common Name: **Dahlia**

A genus of 30 species. Hybridization has resulted in dwarf dahlia cultivars that can be seed propagated and sold as bedding plants. The vast majority of garden plants are cultivars from hybridization between *Dahlia pinnata* and *D. coccinea* grouped together under *D.* x *hybrida*. Much work has been done on shelf life studies of dahlia cuts, but no postharvest research on dwarf dahlia bedding plants is available. Native to Mexico.

DAHL FACE MIX

Production factors

No information available. Using growth regulators (Ancymidol), however, results in more compact plants and better shelf life. Mites and thrips can be serious pests and will affect shelf life.

Postproduction factors

Shipping and handling

Temperature. Plants tolerate a wide temperature range and may be shipped between 50° to 80°F (10° to 27°C). Tubers should be kept between 40° to 45°F (4° to 7°C).

Growth regulators. Using growth regulators such as Ancymidol (A-Rest) will result in more compact growth and thus reduce injury and stress in the postproduction environment.

Retail handling

Light. Low light causes internodal elongation and reduces shelf life.

Temperature. The best shelf life for whole plants is between 50° to 70°F (10° to 21°C). Tubers for sale should be displayed out of the sun in a well-ventilated area and stored in netted bags to allow air circulation or in moist wood shavings.

Irrigation. Dahlias require significant amounts of water; don't let them dry out.

Dahlia

dal-ya

Consumer care

Planting. Break up root balls gently prior to planting.

Location. Plant in full sun in well-drained soil. In the South, dahlias benefit from partial afternoon shade.

Maintenance. To increase plant and flower vigor, remove faded flowers and spray for spider mites. Dahlias are very susceptible to red spotted spider mites.

ADDITIONAL READING

Cathey, H.M. and H.E. Heggestad. 1982. Ozone sensitivity of herbaceous plants: Modification by ethylenediurea. *Journal of the American Society of Horticultural Science* 107(6):1035-1042.

De Hertogh, A.A., N. Blakely and W. Szlachetka. 1976. The influence of ancymidol, chlormequat and daminozide on the growth and development of forced *Dahlia variabilis* wild. *Scientia Hort.* 4:123-130.

Woltering, E.J. and H. Harkema. 1980. *Enige oritnterende waarnemingen omtrent de gevoeligheid van snijbloemen voor ethyleen (II).* (Some data relating cut flower susceptibility to ethylene). *Sprenger Inst. Rep.* 2149: 9 pp.

D

Gomphrena

gom-*free*-na

Family Name: **Amaranthaceae**
Common Name: **Globe Amaranth**

A genus of 100 species. The only species used as a garden plant is *Gomphrena globosa*. Native to tropical America.

BUDDY WHITE

No postproduction information on gomphrena is available, except the following factors:

Production factors

Light. Gomphrena requires high light in the winter months or quality will be reduced and flowering delayed. Decreased production quality will cause reduced shelf life.

Irrigation. Capillary mat watering results in taller plants than those watered by hand; however, additional height doesn't reduce postproduction quality.

Retail handling

Light. At light levels of approximately 100 fc (1.1 klux), flowers persist about 10 days, and foliage remains acceptable for up to 2 weeks.

Consumer care

Location. Plant in full sun. Gomphrena is very heat tolerant and a particularly good species for the South.

Maintenance. Remove faded flowers. An excellent cut flower, gomphrena may be used fresh or dried.

ADDITIONAL READING
Stefanis, J.P. and C.F. Gortzig. 1978. Year-round production of five species of annuals as flowering pot plants. *Florists' Review* 163(4230):22, 64-66.

G

Impatiens

im-*pa*-shenz

Family Name: **Balsaminaceae**
Common Name: **Impatiens**

Impatiens has been the No. 1 best-selling species the last 5 years in the United States, and continued aggressive breeding will assure its future as a leading bedding plant.

SHOWSTOPPER SWEETNESS

Production factors

Light. During winter and early spring production, full light doesn't result in any problems; if production continues into summer, for example, into 4-inch (10-cm) pots, then reduce light by approximately 40% to decrease light intensity and temperature. Stress due to high light and temperature will show up in poorer keeping quality.

Temperature. Temperatures higher than 85°F (29°C) cause continued stress and lessen shelf life. During the final 1 to 2 weeks prior to shipping, you can lower night temperature to 60°F (16°C) but not below 58°F (14°C). Reducing temperatures below 55°F (13°C) can damage foliage and reduce shelf life. Reduce night temperature to 60°F (16°C) at the visible bud stage.

Nutrition. Reduce fertilizer concentration prior to shipping.

Irrigation. Impatiens require copious amounts of water, particularly as temperatures rise. Some wilting may keep plants compact, however. Continued wilting reduces shelf life.

Postproduction factors

Shipping and handling

Light. Impatiens may be shipped in total darkness for up to 36 hours. After 36 hours young flower buds abscise.

Temperature. Don't ship or store below 55°F (13°C).

Gases. Impatiens are highly sensitive to ethylene and even 1 ppm for as little as one hour results in leaf curl; 3 hours causes small flower buds to abcise.

Retail handling

Light. Light intensities of 250 to 700 fc (2.7 to 7.5 klux) are necessary to maintain flowering. This is a wide light range and not difficult to provide. If plants are to be outside, reducing light with shade cloth or other shading is imperative. Impatiens subjected to full sun conditions while in cell

I

packs or small pots decline rapidly. Sixty percent shade is appropriate.

Temperature. Flowers fail to open if temperatures are less than 55°F (13°C) and more than 85°F (29°C). The best range is from 60° to 70°F (16° to 21°C), although no damage has been reported at 55°F (13°C).

Irrigation. Water at the first sign of wilting. Impatiens' high moisture requirement becomes more critical as temperatures grow warmer.

Gases. Impatiens are very sensitive to ethylene and should be displayed away from vehicle traffic. To prevent consumer breakage, don't place impatiens in tiers where people have to reach in to find them; also avoid placing them near corners where they may be bumped or broken.

Grooming. Remove debris whenever possible to prevent disease and ethylene buildup.

Consumer care

Selection. Choose cultivars with suitable heights for the location. For example, tall-growing cultivars like Blitz may be excellent for the Northeast but will fall over in the Southern states.

Location. There are presently no culti vars bred for full sun tolerance. Although some individuals report success growing impatiens in full sun, planting in partial shade makes good garden performance much easier.

Maintenance. Little grooming is required in the garden. Spray for red spider and cyclamen mite if needed. Don't cut plants back unless absolutely necessary.

ADDITIONAL READING

Armitage, A.M. 1982. Keeping quality of bedding plants: Whose responsibility is it? *Florists' Review* 171(4438) 34-35, 39.

Harbaugh, B.K. and W.E. Waters. 1979. Evaluation of flowering potted plants under simulated home conditions. *HortScience* 14(6):743-745

Kowalski, T. and A.M. Armitage. 1982. Effects of light intensity and air temperature on postproduction quality of *Petunia hybrida* and *Impatiens sultanii. HortScience* 17(3):491. Abstr.

Nelson, L.J., A.M. Armitage and W.H. Carlson. Keeping quality of marigolds and impatiens as affected by night temperature and duration. *Florists' Review* 167(4318):28-29, 62, 74.

Nelson, L. and W.H. Carlson. 1987. Improve the marketability of bedding plants. *Greenhouse Grower* 5(3):84-85

Reid, M.S. 1981. Silver thiosulfate (STS) may prevent losses during transportation of flowering potted plants. *Hort Crops Perish. Hand.* 48:8

Sullivan, G.H., J.L. Robertson and G.L. Staby. 1980. Post-harvest losses during transportation of nursery stock and bedding plants. *Management for retail florists with applications to nursery and garden centers.* Ch 24: 505-525.

Lobularia

Family Name: **Brassicaceae**
Common Name: **Alyssum**

A genus of a single species, *Lobularia maritima*.

EASTER BONNET MIX

There's no postproduction information available except the following:

Production factors

Soils. In soil studies, no difference occurred in shelf life between plants grown in a soil-based vs. a peat-lite medium.

Postproduction factors

Shipping and storage

Light. Darkness will stop alyssum from flowering within 36 hours.

Temperature. Alyssum tolerates tem-peratures as low as 40°F (4°C).

Gases. Alyssum plants are relatively insensitive to ethylene.

Seedling storage. Seedlings ready for transplanting may be stored up to 6 weeks. Although not recommended, seedlings may be stored up to 2 weeks. When seedlings have reached the proper transplanting stage, water containers thoroughly. After excess water has drained, place containers in polyethylene bags, and seal the bags with rubber bands. Store them in a 35° to 40°F (2° to 4°C) refrigerator, 12 inches (30 cm) below fluorescent lamps. Keep lights on 14 hours daily.

Retail handling

Light. Provide as much light as possible in the retail environment. Alyssum should have a minimum light intensity of 700 fc (7.5 klux). This is approximately 60% to 70% shade if marketed outdoors.

Temperature. Cooling through ventila-tion and shading is beneficial as warm temperatures cause reduced shelf life. Temperatures of 40° to 55°F (4° to 13°C) are optimum.

Grooming. Clean up alyssum if plants are damaged, but it's less sensitive to wear and tear than many other species.

L

Lobularia

lob-yew-*lah*-re-a

Consumer care

Planting. Break up soil ball before planting in ground.

Location. Place plants in full sun in the North. In the South they perform better in partial shade.

Maintenance. Alyssum requires little maintenance, although it's moderately susceptible to spider mites.

ADDITIONAL READING

Nelson, L. and W.H. Carlson. 1987. Improve the marketability of bedding plants. *Greenhouse Grower* 5(3):84-85.

Nelson, L.E. 1984. "The influence of environmental factors on postproduction keeping quality of bedding plants." M.S. thesis, Michigan State University.

L

Pelargonium

pe-lar-*gon*-ee-um

Family Name: **Geraniaceae**
Common Name: **Geranium**

The genus consists of over 250 species; bedding geraniums belong to the group known as *Pelargonium* × *hortorum*.

BRAZIL

Production factors

Light. Grow geraniums with as much light as possible during the winter and spring months to obtain high quality plants. Light may be slightly reduced at visible bud without flower quality loss.

Temperature. From visible bud onset until flowers open, lower temperatures to reduce petal shatter. If it's impossible to ship plants as they reach full flower stage, attempt to hold plants between 40° to 55°F (4° to 13°C) or petals will fall. Ethylene doesn't form as rapidly under low temperatures.

Growth regulators. Use growth regulators such as A-Rest, Bonzi and Cycocel on medium- and tall-growing cultivars for more compact, better quality plants. This also slightly enhances shelf life.

Gases. Ethylene causes petal shatter, and anything that reduces ethylene concentration minimizes damage. Application of 1mM silver thiosulfate (STS) when flowers begin to show color significantly reduces petal shatter. Just prior to STS application, spray against *Pythium ultimum* (a common soil water mold), as STS makes plants much more susceptible to root rot caused by this organism.

Postproduction factors

The biggest problem associated with seed-propagated geraniums is susceptibility to petal shatter. Environmental conditions that cause plant stress and the subsequent ethylene production speed up this natural phenomenon. The best way to solve this problem is to ship plants before the flowers open. Although it's not always possible, this should be the aim of all geranium growers who ship more than 10 miles. Vegetatively propagated geraniums don't suffer from

P

petal shatter; however, both geranium types suffer from leaf yellowing (chlorosis) during shipping.

Shipping, handling and storage

Light. Darkness itself doesn't promote shattering, but any additional stress can result in additional shatter. Darkness, however, can cause leaf chlorosis when plants remain in shipping containers longer than 48 hours.

Temperature. Geraniums ship better at 40°F (4°C) than at 75°F (24°C), and this is especially true if ethylene is present. Low temperatures offset ethylene's detrimental effects—leaf yellowing and petal shatter.

Gases. Ethylene is obviously a problem, causing both leaf chlorosis and petal shatter. Low light, high temperatures and rough handling during transportation will raise ethylene levels and shorten shelf life.

Cutting storage. Few garden geraniums are propagated from cuttings; however, large numbers of rooted and unrooted cuttings are used in producing vegetatively propagated geraniums. Often these cuttings must be stored as well as shipped long distances.

Light. Geranium cuttings are normally stored in humidified containers in darkness.

Temperature. Cuttings can be placed in refrigerated storage at 41°F (5°C) and 95% humidity. Store unrooted cuttings approximately 2 weeks and rooted cuttings for about 3 weeks with this system.

Atmospheric pressure. Low pressure storage (LPS) facilities that use reduced atmospheric pressure (usually around one-tenth normal atmosphere), low temperature and high humidity can extend unrooted cutting storage time by 3 to 4 weeks and rooted cuttings by 2 weeks.

Disease control. If cuttings are to be stored, it's essential to provide some fungal pathogen control. Dip cuttings in a fungicide and allow them to dry before storing.

Retail handling

Light. Inside the retail outlet, provide geraniums with as much light as possible. If they're placed outside, use shade cloth or other means to reduce light by at least 50%. If geraniums are sold in 4- or 6-inch (10- or 15-cm) containers, providing light is less of a problem than when sold in cell packs. Regardless of their container, provide geraniums with some shade.

Temperature. Low temperature (below 45°F [7°C]) will redden geranium foliage. A little reddening enhances leaf zonation, but continued exposure to low temperatures causes blotchy, sad-looking foliage. Warm temperatures (above 85°F [20°C]) cause excessive drying out of the soil and chlorotic leaves. Use ventilation and shading to reduce temperature.

Irrigation. Geraniums don't show water stress by wilting as do impatiens. Because their leaves are thicker, wilting is one of geraniums' last responses. This means that plants may be under significant water stress before it's noticed. Leaves that require water will be a little limp around the margins and usually light green, with little zonation. Water plants as needed to reduce this.

Grooming. It's essential to remove dead and dying tissue from geraniums to reduce any ethylene buildup. Remove spent flower heads from both vegetatively and seed-propagated plants.

P

Pelargonium

Consumer care

Location. Seed-propagated cultivars are best suited for ground bed displays, whereas the larger-flowered, vegetatively propagated cultivars are magnificent in containers and deck and patio planters. This is certainly not a hard and fast rule—any geranium may be used in any sunny area. Geraniums don't do well in partial or full shade, however.

Maintenance. Removing faded flower heads is necessary to keep plants blooming through the summer. Adding a complete fertilizer as well as an iron application will greatly improve geranium garden performance.

ADDITIONAL READING

Armitage, A.M., R. Heins, S. Dean and W. Carlson. 1980. Factors influencing flower petal abscission in the seed-propagated geranium. *Journal of the American Society of Horticultural Science* 105(4):562-564.

Cameron, A.C. and M.S. Reid. 1981. The use of silver thiosulfate anionic complex as a foliar spray. II. Prevention of shattering in potted geraniums. *HortScience* 16(3):405. Abstract.

———. Use of silver thiosulfate to prevent flower abscission from potted plants. *Scientia Horticultura* 19(3-4):373-378.

———. 1983. STS can prevent flower shattering in some pot plants. *Greenhouse Manager* 2(1):40, 42-43.

Carlson, W.H. 1982. STS eliminates petal shattering. *Florists' Review* 170(4409):150-152.

Dean, S. and W.H. Carlson. 1979. Effect of ethylene on the shipment of seed geraniums (*Pelargonium* x *hortorum* Bailey). *HortScience* 14(3):444-445.

Eisenberg, B.A., G. L. Staby and T.A. Fretz. 1978. Low pressure and refrigerated storage of rooted and unrooted ornamental cuttings. *Journal of the American Society of Horticultural Science* 3(6):732-737.

———. 1979. Low pressure and refrigerated storage of rooted and unrooted ornamental cuttings. *Florists' Review* 165(4269):104-105, 119-123.

Gruber, J. and B.A. Eisenberg. 1984. Improving the quality of unrooted *Pelargonium* x *hortorum* cuttings during shipping with improved handling procedures. *HortScience* 19(3):560.

Harbaugh, B.K. and W.E. Waters. 1979. Evaluation of flowering potted plants under simulated home conditions. *HortScience* 14(6):743-745.

Hausbeck, M.K., C.T. Stevens and R. Heins. 1984. Increased *Pythium ultimum* induced mortality on geranium by application of silver thiosulfate. *HortScience* 19(3):570.

Heins, R. and H. Fonda. 1983. Mixing STS. *Bedding Plants Inc. News* 19(5):6.

Marousky, F.J. and B.K. Harbaugh. 1981. Influence of temperature, light, and ethylene on seedlings of geranium (*Pelargonium* x *hortorum* Bailey) during simulated shipping conditions. *Journal of the American Society of Horticultural Science* 106(5):527-530.

Miranda, R. and W.H. Carlson. 1981. How to stop petal shattering in seed propagated geraniums. *GrowerTalks* 45(7):18-22.

P

Perennials

Many species are presently grown for mail order, retail and wholesale markets. Perennials grown for bedding plant spring trade should be planted in 3- to 4-inch (7-cm) pots and treated like cold-tolerant annuals. Some species are sold bare root from the field, others are potted and handled like any other pot crop.

Potted perennials

If perennials are shipped green (without flower), postproduction problems on flowers will be minimal. Perennials forced in flower in 4-inch (10-cm) or larger pots should be marketed in early spring. Maintain cool temperatures prior to shipping to reduce plant stretch and flower abscission. Information concerning postproduction of annuals applies to perennial species also. Maintaining cool temperatures is more critical with most perennial species because they're grown cool. Warm temperatures (greater than 65°F [18°C]) in the retail outlet cause stretched plants and yellow basal leaves, especially if they're allowed to dry out.

Bare root shipments

The following information is based on work by Arthur Cameron and his students, Ralph Heiden and Muhammad Maqbool, at Michigan State University.

Producer

Storage. Remove excess soil and store at 28° to 32°F (-2° to 0°C) in polyethylene bags until plants are shipped. Using refrigerated trucks is preferable, although perennials are also transported in unrefrigerated trucks.

Grower

Upon delivery. Inspect for crown and root surface mold, internal rot or shriveled and dry plants. If these conditions are present, regrowth may be poor. A small amount of surface mold is usually only unsightly and has little or no effect on regrowth. When surface molds cover less than 50% of the roots, crowns or foliage, there's no effect on subsequent regrowth. When mold covers more than 50%, however, regrowth is poor.

Moisture loss. If it's necessary to store bare-root material when received, don't let plants dry out. For every 1% weight loss, plants show corresponding reduction in regrowth quality of 1% to 2%. Species such as *Phlox subulata* tolerate up to 10% loss of fresh weight before showing a decline in regrowth quality. Minimize water loss by storing or covering bare-root plants in 4 mil polyethylene bags. When cooling roots, reduce condensation in crates and bags by lowering temperatures to 32° to 37°F (0° to 3°C) and providing good air circulation. Storing roots below 41°F (5°C) will result in minimal regrowth decline. Avoid temperature fluctuations as these result in condensate around the crown or roots—a good growing base for mold.

P

Perennials

ADDITIONAL READING

Mahlstede, T.P. and W.E. Fletcher. 1960. Storage of nursery stock. *American Association of Nurserymen*, Washington, DC.

Heiden, R. and A.C. Cameron. 1986. Bare-root perennials require cautious handling. *American Nurseryman* 163(7):75-78.

Heiden, Ralph W. 1987. "The effect of post storage temperatures and freeze/thaw cycles on regrowth performance of bare-root herbaceous perennials." M.S. thesis, Michigan State University.

Maqbool, Muhammad. 1986. "Postharvest handling and storage of bare-root herbaceous perennials." M.S. thesis, Michigan State University.

P

Petunia

pe-*tewn*-ee-a

Family Name: **Solanaceae**
Common Name: **Petunia**

A genus of approximately 30 annual or perennial species. The commercially important member is *Petunia* x *hybrida* resulting from hybridization of *Petunia axillaris, P. inflata* and *P. violacea*. Various horticultural names attached to petunias such as multiflora, grandiflora and nana are not species or cultivars but descriptive terms of flower or plant habit.

FALCON WHITE

Production factors

Light. Grow plants in full sun during winter and spring. Low light intensity causes internode stretching.

Temperature. To increase longevity, reduce temperatures when buds are visible. Reducing night temperature from 60° to 50°F (16° to 10°C) adds to postproduction longevity. It must be understood, however, that reducing temperature at visible bud will also delay flower opening. It's necessary to add this additional time to the original flowering schedule.

Nutrition. Reducing nitrogen nutrition from visible bud until flowering helps longevity under many temperature ranges.

Decrease nitrogen by 50% (for example, from 200 to 100 ppm nitrogen) at this time. Don't totally stop nitrogen applications because this will reduce shelf life.

Container. A larger container holding more medium will provide better water retention, desirable in mass market longevity.

Irrigation. Reducing the water applied to plants helps them last longer. Cut back on water from the visible bud stage until flowers open. Allowing soil to become dry between waterings, even if slight wilting occurs, won't reduce quality and will enhance longevity, particularly if plants will be sold in warm or hot areas.

Specific chemical application. Growth retardants don't necessarily increase longevity, but if plants are too tall for their containers, then shelf life will suffer. Petunias are very sensitive to ozone and sulfur dioxide pollutants; if damage occurs during the production phase, shelf life will be decreased. Daminozide (B-Nine) is registered for use as an anti-air-pollution chemical on petunia and is effective if used during the last stages of production if plants are to be exposed to those pollutants in high amounts.

P

Petunia

Postproduction factors

Shipping, handling and storage

No data are available on transporting petunias, but since they tolerate full sun conditions, leaves of plants shipped in the dark would likely yellow within 3 to 4 days as does geranium foliage. Since flowering petunias stored at 50°F (10°C) had better shelf life than those stored at 70°F (21°C) or higher, shipping temperatures of 50°F would probably be acceptable for petunias. Lower temperatures might cause even greater longevity since petunia is a very cold-tolerant species.

Seedling storage. Although not recommended, seedlings may be stored up to 2 weeks. When seedlings have reached the proper transplanting stage, water containers thoroughly. After excess water has drained, place containers in polyethylene bags, and seal the bags with rubber bands. Store them in a 35° to 40°F (2° to 4°C) refrigerator, 12 inches (30 cm) below fluorescent lamps. Keep lights on 14 hours daily. Seedlings can be stored this way for four to six weeks.

Retail handling

Light. Even though petunias are high-light plants, shading plants helps them last longer by reducing temperature and therefore water loss. Shading isn't that important if plants will be retailed at cool temperatures (50° to 60°F [10° to 16°C]), but the warmer the retail temperatures, the more important shading becomes.

Temperature. Reducing temperature is probably the most important environmental change that can be made at the retail level.

For many plants such as petunia, the optimum temperature is around 50°F (10°C), but that's often hard to control if spring temperatures start to rise. At temperatures approaching 90°F (32°C), plants will first stretch and then quickly lose all remaining quality within 5 to 7 days.

Irrigation. The single greatest reason for bedding plant decline is lack of water. Small container volume combined with warm temperatures in retail areas often causes plants to dry out rapidly—without adequate replacement water, plants simply decline. Petunias' wilting pattern isn't as clear as that of some other species, and sometimes people don't think they need water, even when dry. Watering once in the morning is usually inadequate, especially with cell packs.

Consumer care

Planting. Break up soil ball before planting in order to mix greenhouse and garden soils.

Location. Petunias perform best when planted in full sun.

Maintenance. Petunias can be cut back after flowering, especially grandiflora types. In southern states, plants not cut back will develop elongated stems and flowering will stop, leaving the consumer with a sickly, scraggly foliage plant. All U.S. retailers should recommend hard pruning after flowering.

P

Petunia

pe-*tewn*-ee-a

ADDITIONAL READING

Armitage, A.M. and T. Kowalski. 1983. Effect of irrigation frequency during greenhouse production on the postproduction quality of *Petunia hybrida* Vilm. *Journal of the American Society of Horticultural Science* 108(1):118-121.

Armitage, A.M. and T. Kowalski. 1983. Effects of light intensity and air temperature in simulated postproduction environment on *Petunia hybrida* Vilm. *Journal of the American Society of Horticultural Science* 108(1):115-118.

Boodley, J.W., A. Bing, T.C. Weiler, L. Albright, M. Daughtrey, M. Semel and L. Topoleski. 1984. Storage of seedlings. *Cornell Bedding Plant Guidelines for N.Y. State* 1984:5.

Brooks, W.M., H.K. Tayama, R.K. Lindquist, C.C. Powell, J. Peterson, W.R. Faber and J.L. Robertson. 1982. Seedling storage. *Tips on Growing Bedding Plants.* Columbus: Ohio State University.

Cathey, H.M. and H.E. Heggestad. 1982. Ozone and sulfur dioxide sensitivity of petunia: Modification by ethylenediurea. *Journal of the American Society of Horticultural Science* 107(6):1028-1035.

Fischer, C.W. 1950. Ethylene gas a problem in cut flower storage. *N.Y. State Flower Growers Bulletin* 61:1, 4.

Gehring, J.M. 1979. "Shelf life extension of bedding plants." M.S. thesis, Virginia Polytech. Institute.

Gilissen, L.J.W. 1977. Style-controlled wilting of the flower. *Planta* 133:275-280.

Harbaugh, B.K. and W.E. Waters. 1979. Evaluation of flowering potted plants under simulated home conditions. *HortScience* 14(6):743-745.

Jeffcoat, B. 1977. Influence of the cytokinin, 6-benzylamino-9-Otetrahydropyran-2-YL)-9H-purine, on the growth and development of some ornamental crops. *J. Hort. Sci.* 52(1):143-153.

Kowalski, T. and A.M. Armitage. 1982. Effects of light intensity and air temperature on postproduction quality of *Petunia hybrida* and *Impatiens sultanii*. *HortScience* 17(3):491. Abstract.

Wise, F.C. and W.C. Fonteno. Effects of growth regulators on postproduction performance of Happiness petunias. *HortScience* 15(3):389-390.

P

Salvia

sal-vee-a

Family Name: **Labiatae**
Common Name: **Salvia**

A large genus of more than 750 species of herbs, subshrubs and shrubs. *Salvia splendens*, **scarlet sage, is the main commercially produced annual salvia but** *S. farinacea*, **mealycup sage, and** *S. coccinea*, **flaming sage, are also grown as bedding plants. The most popular perennial species being produced is the purple-flowered** *S.* x *superba*.

SCARLET KING

Production factors

Nutrition. Plants are heavy feeders (300 ppm constant liquid feed). Cut fertilizer in half 1 to 2 weeks prior to sale.

Container. Using a deeper container significantly enhances shelf life. Increasing container depth from 2 to 4 inches (5 to 10 cm) can increase shelf life by 42%.

Postproduction factors

Shipping, handling and storage
No information on environmental effects during transportation is available for salvia except the following:

Gases. Salvia is very ethylene sensitive—ventilate and cool the staging area and delivery vehicles.

Seedling storage. Although not recommended, seedlings may be stored up to 2 weeks. When seedlings have reached the proper transplanting stage, water containers thoroughly. After excess water has drained, place containers in polyethylene bags, and seal the bags with rubber bands. Store them in a 35° to 40°F (2° to 4°C) refrigerator, 12 inches (30 cm) below fluorescent lamps. Keep lights on 14 hours daily. Salvia seedlings can be successfully stored this way for 4 to 6 weeks.

Retail handling

When tested as a potted plant for indoor use, flowers abscised after 2 weeks, but foliage remained acceptable for 4 weeks. Light was approximately 100 fc (1.1 klux) for 12 hours and temperature was 73° to 80°F (23° to 27°C). It's important to provide an ethylene-free environment through proper grooming and ventilation.

S

Salvia

sal-vee-a

Consumer care

Location. In the North, salvia tolerates full sun, but in the South, afternoon shade is best.

Fertilization. Fertilize plants two to three times with a complete fertilizer within 2 weeks of planting.

Maintenance. Remove faded flowers to ensure constant flowering.

ADDITIONAL READING

Boodley, J.W., A. Bing, T.C. Weiler, L. Albright, M. Daughtrey, M. Semel and L. Topoleski. 1984. Storage of seedlings. *Cornell Bedding Plant Guidelines for N.Y. State.*

Gehring, J.M. and A.J. Lewis. 1979. Extending the shelf life of bedding plants, I. Container volume. *Florists' Review* 165(4278):17, 60-61.

Harbaugh, B.K. and W.E. Waters. 1979. Evaluation of flowering potted plants under simulated home conditions. *HortScience* 14(6):743-745.

Nelson, L. and W.H. Carlson. 1987. Improve the marketability of bedding plants. *Greenhouse Grower* 5(3):84-85.

S

Tagetes

ta-*gay*-teez

Family Name: **Asteraceae**
Common Name: **Marigold**

There are approximately 30 marigold species but the two most commonly cultivated are *Tagetes erecta*, African marigolds, and *T. patula,* French marigolds.
Aggressive breeding programs have created a tremendous number of cultivars,
including triploids, with parentage becoming more difficult to determine.

HERO FLAME, RED AND GOLD

Production factors

Temperature. Reducing night temperature to 50°F (10°C) for at least 1 week prior
to sale adds nearly 1 week additional shelf
life.

Nutrition. Reducing fertilizer frequency
and/or concentration once the bud is visible
also adds additional shelf life.

Container. As with ageratum, salvia and
zinnia, increasing marigold's container
depth from 2 to 4 inches (5 to 10 cm) can
significantly increase shelf life.

Soil amendments. Research work has
shown that incorporating 5 ½ pounds of
hydrogel per cubic yard (8 kg per cubic m)
into the medium can lengthen marigold's
shelf life.

Postproduction factors

Shipping, handling and storage
Light. Placing plants in the dark for 4
days causes smaller flowers and leaves. No
flower or leaf abscission occurs up to 7 days
and height increases caused by reduced light
is minimal.

Gases. Marigold is relatively insensitive
to ethylene, requiring 48 hours exposure to
10 ppm before leaves begin to droop. It's
moderately sensitive to ozone.

Seedling storage. Seedlings may be kept
up to 6 weeks in refrigerated storage.
Although not recommended, seedlings may
be stored up to 2 weeks. When seedlings
have reached the proper transplanting stage,
water containers thoroughly. After excess
water has drained, place containers in
polyethylene bags, and seal the bags with
rubber bands. Store them in a 35° to 40°F
(2° to 4°C) refrigerator, 12 inches (30 cm)
below fluorescent lamps. Keep lights on 14
hours daily.

T

Tagetes

ta-*gay*-teez

Retail handling

Light. Provide as much light as possible in the retail store, but 50% to 60% shade for plants marketed outside. Although some French marigold cultivars continue to flower for over 2 weeks at approximately 100 fc (1.1 klux), some cultivars stop flowering entirely after 1 week.

Temperature. Reduce temperature as close to 50°F (10°C) as possible. Temperatures above 85°F (29°C) will stretch plants; those dipping below 50°F will cause the foliage to redden.

Grooming. Marigolds are tough plants, tolerating rough handling better than most other bedding plants. Broken flowers and damaged leaves must be removed, however, because ethylene from these plant parts will affect more sensitive species nearby.

Consumer care

Planting. Break up soil ball in preparation for planting.

Location. Plant marigolds in full sun.

Maintenance. Remove faded and dead flowers to keep plants blooming. Marigolds are highly susceptible to Botrytis and spider mite infestations.

ADDITIONAL READING

Armitage, A.M. 1982. Keeping quality of bedding plants. Whose responsibility is it? *Florists' Review* 171(4438):34-35, 39.

Boodley, J.W. A. Bing, T. C. Weiler, L. Albright, M. Daughtrey, M. Semel and L. Topoleski. 1984. Storage of seedlings. *Cornell Bedding Plant Guidelines for NY State* 1984:5.

Cathey, H.M. and H.E. Heggestad. 1982. Ozone sensitivity of herbaceous plants: Modification by ethylenediurea. *Journal American Society Horticultural Science* 107(6):1035-1042.

Gehring, J.M., and A.J. Lewis. 1979. Extending the shelf life of bedding plants. I. Container volume. *Florists' Review* 165(4278):17, 60-61.

———. 1980. Effect of hydrogel on wilting and moisture stress of bedding plants. *Journal of the American Society of Horticultural Science* 105(4):511-513.

Harbaugh, B.K. and W.E. Waters. 1979. Evaluation of flowering potted plants under simulated home conditions. *HortScience* 14(6):743-745.

Neff, M.S. and W.E. Loomis. 1935. Storage of French marigolds. *Proc. Amer. Soc. Hort. Sci.* 33:683-685.

Nelson, L.E., A.M. Armitage and W.H. Carlson. 1980. Keeping quality of marigolds and impatiens as affected by night temperature and duration. *Florists' Review* 167(4318):28-29, 62, 74.

Nelson, L. and W.H. Carlson. 1987. Improving the marketability of bedding plants. *Greenhouse Grower* 5(3):84-85.

T

Zinnia

zin-ee-a

Family Name: **Asteraceae**
Common Name: **Zinnia**

A genus of approximately 17 species. The major species in the greenhouse trade is *Zinnia elegans*. *Z. angustifolia* (*Z. linearis*) has great potential.

PETER PAN MIX

Production factors

Growth regulators. Many zinnia cultivars require growth regulators for height control, especially if grown in cell packs or small containers. If growth regulators aren't used and plants are floppy when sold, they decline rapidly upon reaching the retail outlet.

Container. As with many other bedding plants, additional container depth for zinnias means additional shelf life. Research showed a 39% increase in shelf life for plants in 4-inch deep (10 cm) compared with 2-inch deep (5 cm) containers.

Soil amendments. Incorporating hydrogel at 5½ pounds per cubic yard (8 kg per cubic m) significantly increases shelf life.

Postproduction factors

Transportation, shipping and storage
   Gases. Zinnia isn't ethylene sensitive.
   Seedling storage. Zinnia seedlings don't store well and must be transplanted at the proper stage of development.

Retail handling

Light. As with other species, shading for zinnias is necessary if plants are marketed outdoors. If displayed in a shop, give them as much light as possible. Flowers fade rapidly at low light (100 fc [1.1 klux]) levels.

Temperature. Zinnias don't tolerate cool temperatures well, and temperatures below 50°F (10°C) should be avoided.

Irrigation. Zinnias often enter the retail area with minor leaf infections that don't show up unless plants are stressed. Sloppy watering that splashes soil and soaks leaves worsens the infections—particularly evident when temperatures are hot.

Z

67

Bedding Plants *Zinnia*

Zinnia

zin-ee-a

Consumer care

Planting. Break up soil ball in preparation for planting.

Location. Plant in full sun, but irrigate well when first planted. Zinnias are very heat tolerant.

Maintenance. Spray programs to control leaf-spotting fungi should be started in July. Better resistance is being bred in some of the newer *Z. elegans* and *Z. angustifolia* cultivars, so no spraying is necessary. Remove faded flowers to prolong blooming.

ADDITIONAL READING

Boodley, J.W., A. Bing, T.C. Weiler, L. Albright, M. Daughtrey, M. Semel and L. Topoleski. 1984. Storage of Seedlings. *Cornell Bedding Plant Guidelines for New York State* 1984:5.

Gehring, J.M. and A.J. Lewis. 1979. Extending the shelf life of bedding plants. I. Container volume. *Florists' Review* 165(4278):17, 60-61.

————. 1979. Extending the shelf life of bedding plants. II. Hydrogel. *Florists' Review* 165(4282):30, 46.

————. 1980. Extending the shelf life of bedding plants. III. Antitranspirants. *Florists' Review* 165(4286):31, 65.

Harbaugh, B.K. and W.E. Waters. 1979. Evaluation of flowering potted plants under simulated home conditions. *HortScience* 14(6):743-745.

Stefanis, J.P. and C.F. Gortzig. 1978. Year round production of 5 species of annuals as flowering bedding plants. *Florists' Review* 163(4230):22, 64-66.

Z

GLOSSARY

Abscission. Dropping of buds, flowers or leaves. May be caused either by mechanical or environmental factors.

Antitranspirant. A substance generally sprayed on the foliage to reduce loss of water from the leaves.

Bedding plant. Plants generally, but not always, grown from seed and designed to be planted outdoors in beds or containers. Usually thought of as ornamental species; however, vegetables, like tomatoes and peppers are often included in a bedding plant mix.

Cultivar. A cultivated variety. Most common bedding plant cultivars are hybrids and are produced from seed. The seed developed from these plants, however, will produce the same cultivar when sown.

Ethylene. An odorless, colorless gas which may be produced by damaged tissue, automobiles, or ripening fruit. Exposure to ethylene generally results in negative effects, such as reduced shelf life, bud abscission and flower shattering.

Growth regulators. Chemicals applied to bedding plants that are generally, but not always, used to regulate height.

Grooming. Removing dead or damaged leaves and flowers from plants both prior to shipping and in the sales area.

Hormone. A growth regulator naturally produced by the plant.

Hydrophilic polymer. A water-absorbing substance incorporated into the media to reduce irrigation frequency.

mM (millimolar). A measurement used in preparing silver thiosulfate (STS).

Petal shatter. A condition usually associated with seed-propagated geraniums in which the flower petals abscise. This is a natural condition that may be relieved by cool temperatures or applying silver thiosulfate (STS).

Plug. A term used to describe single plant transplants. The number of plugs varies from fewer than 100 to 800 per standard tray. Plugs are transplanted to final containers for finishing.

ppm (parts per million). A unit of measure in chemical concentrations. One ppm equals 1 mg of a pure substance in 1 liter of water. (One ounce of pure substance in 100 gallons of water equals 75 ppm of that substance.)

Precooling. A procedure to rapidly cool plants or flowers prior to shipping in order to prevent stress during shipping.

Quality. The appearance and/or value of bedding plants. Quality considerations are size, flower number, freedom from insect, disease or mechanical damage.

Shelf life. The length of time from production in the greenhouse until plants no longer meet the aesthetic demands of the consumer.

STS (silver thiosulfate). STS is applied to geraniums to reduce petal shatter by inhibiting ethylene activity. Because of silver's permanence in the environment, handle STS with care and dispose properly.

Toning. Procedures used to prepare plants for the postproduction environment.

Visible bud. The stage of flower development when the flower bud is just visible to the naked eye. Treatments for plant toning often begin at this stage.

CROP INDEX